Countercultural
Woman

Mimi Elles

ISBN 978-1-0980-6437-2 (paperback)
ISBN 978-1-0980-6438-9 (digital)

Christian Faith Publishing, Inc.
832 Park Avenue
Meadville, PA 16335
www.christianfaithpublishing.com

Author Photo by photographer Elliot Morales

Printed in the United States of America

Acknowledgment

In gratitude and praise to God for speaking to me through my Mamu, my aunt Karla, Libia, and many wonderful women in my life; for showing me His truth, and for the opportunity to share it.

In love, to Derek, my great husband, because his love and patience have challenged me to be the woman God wants for him: a virtuous woman. My special gratitude for his great, unconditional support, his patience, and understanding in trying to figure out my heart and soul to help me go through each stage this book has taken, for his great interest in detail and precision in the translation process.

In faith, to my nephews Fabio and Diego. May the Lord bring into each of your lives a virtuous woman who knows how to treat you as men of God, because that is what I trust the Lord will do for you. I love you.

To my dear friends Kim Slowinski and Jean Herg, for their support to my ministry, my family, myself, and this book. Your contributions matter so much, thank you!

To my sweet Berta Abrego, for her contribution to the Spanish edition. It is my joy to see you grow and become a wonderful woman of God.

Introduction

There have been many books, conferences, talks, and Bible studies about the virtuous woman that express her excellence in such a way that it can be intimidating and even annoying. We prefer not to know much about her so as to avoid comparing her to ourselves and feeling bad. After all, who can be that excellent in everything? I definitely cannot.

Many Christian women today say things to the effect, "She is one of those women from long ago, a time past, things have changed since those times. Yes, it is true that she is in the Bible, but I am a millennial. All that is not for me. It has nothing to do with me. She is one of those women who are at home taking care of their children and who do not have professional careers."

They seem to believe that not only does this woman not follow the standards of modern women, but she is a woman whose life does not appear to flourish in ways that today's culture celebrates. However, the Bible teaches us much more about her and why she is such an example for women not only in every culture but also in every generation.

Nowadays, there are many women who are leaving their homes to go out and work and grow as professionals. Many, in fact, do not have children, nor do they plan on having them. While we think about these women, others have left their professional careers to become mothers: to stay home and take care of their families. Among these women, some feel frustrated because they believe they are wasting their potential by putting their efforts into mundane, daily tasks such as washing clothes, house cleaning, and cooking.

No matter what you are doing, leaving home or staying, there is a great truth for you in the model of the virtuous woman, which God has called us all to be. It is my prayer that within the pages of this book, you will realize this calling and start working toward it. Perhaps you already realize this, but you need a little push, in which case I hope this book provides that thrust.

Throughout this book, you will find information, explanations, challenges, and applications for your life that I am sure will help you get on and maintain your path to fullness. While many have written on this subject, this is the compilation of my own study and my years of experience working with women of different countries, from rural and urban areas, and of all ages. It is a process of learning and trans-formations. Some things are easier than others, but in each one, God will be by your side. Keep reading; even if you feel that the topic does not apply to your life, it does apply, I promise you!

There is no condemnation here as none of us is or will be 100 percent. After all the research, applications, testimonials, reading, and writing, I am not 100 percent—but I continue toward the goal. In the end, that is the biggest challenge: that we will always be in the process of growth for a fullness of life in Christ.

My desire is to clarify some misconceived ideas, present the implications, and show the privilege of being a homemaker. With this, I want to tell you—and here we begin—that at some point of every day, we are all homemakers, and we should all be homemakers.

You will see that I do not quote any authors for reference inso-much as my desire is that you find fullness in the Word and not in the well-spoken sayings of renowned writers. For this reason, I have only used biblical references in hopes of bringing the truth of God into your heart.

The virtuous woman lives fully in every aspect of her life. She manages her every day in such a way as to feel accomplished, moving toward a fullness of life that can be found only in Christ and only when we submit to the path of good works that He prepared for us a long time ago.

The challenge I encountered when I started learning about the vir-tuous woman was to live life fully, not only as a woman but as a Christian woman. This challenge changed the way I think, feel, live, and praise, taking me to the feet of Christ where there is true fullness. In my daily walk with Christ, I come closer and closer to that fullness that is in Him, and my prayer is that this book will guide you to the same.

The Virtuous Woman

The passage from Proverbs 31:10–31 comprises a list of virtues that a mother gives her son to look for in a wife. In other words, this mother is not describing an actual person but is advising her son of the characteristics to look for in whom he will take to be his wife. It is not evident in current translations, but in the original Bible language, the characteristics are written as an acrostic, which uses the letters of the Hebrew alphabet, because it is a pleasant and easy method of memorization. This mother really knows the importance of a good wife and, therefore, goes the great lengths to make sure that her son knows how to identify her.

Knowing this, we can say that there is no machismo influence as this was not born of a male chauvinist who wishes to perpetuate male dominance. No! It was born in the heart of a woman and more so of a mother who wants the best for her son, for her grandchildren, for her family. Who doesn't want the best for their family?

It needs to be clarified here that this mother is not matriarchal. Her counsel is not only aimed at the excellence of the ideal woman but also to the good conduct and behavior of an important man. This mother's son is a king, King Lemuel, and she tells him, in the first verses of the same chapter, about the proper conduct of a king in such basic and general terms that every man should seek direction in them.

Knowing more about the context of our passage, we see that the virtuous woman is the right woman for a king. Who will find her?

It is like searching for a needle in a haystack. But whoever finds her finds a treasure.

So the virtuous woman does not exist. She is a paradigm, an ideal, a challenge for all women to pursue. This archetype, however, gives us all the opportunity to hit the sought-after mark. Each woman, in her own way and context, can achieve the excellence desired by a king: a queen worthy of praise.

It Really Doesn't Matter

Our society has had its values upside down for a long time. We have validated the wrong and given importance to what is not transcendent. A woman confident of herself is a better role model than a woman fearful of God, and the church has done little to undo this confusion. Society's ideals of success and beauty set standards unreachable for most women and which are far from what the Lord deems as value in a woman (1 Peter 3:1–4).

The Bible focuses its teachings on the elements that produce true worth in a woman and a standard which is attainable by each of them. While this book focuses on these biblical teachings, I want us to feel freedom in the Lord by knowing what things do not matter so that we get rid of prejudices and pressures imposed by a society that does not glorify God or give Him thanks (Romans 1:21).

Academy

An academic degree does not guarantee education and proper behavior, nor is it a requirement to be a woman of worth. Not to say that it is bad for women to be educated, cultivating their minds, or better that they do not pursue knowledge at all. Despite your effort in academics, in the workplace, or in your success as a professional, there are duties of the home that are your responsibility, and you must do them as for the Lord: with joy and excellence (Colossians 3:17, 23; 1 Corinthians 10:31).

Nothing is mentioned in the Bible about the educational level of the virtuous woman because it really doesn't matter.

Age

According to the marriage practices depicted in the Old Testament, it could be assumed that the virtuous woman is very young. However, due to her many virtues, she may be older since many of them come with experience through age. Whatever your age, whether you have been married for a long time or you are a newlywed, being a dignified, honorable woman is always important. You will not have wasted years by not being one; neither will you waste years by being one. It is an exercise of the soul and a lifelong process to achieve all these qualities. The important thing is to start.

If you are single, you still have a family whom you can honor in such a way that they are witnesses of your dignity. Your parents, your nieces and nephews, your friends, your coworkers, and your church congregation will see this idealized woman made reality in you for the glory of God.

The virtuous woman's age, we do not know. What we do know is that since the Bible does not mention or make reference to it, it really doesn't matter.

Size

Beauty is important in all cultures, but the concept of beauty changes not only from one culture to another but from person to person within each culture. This mother of a king is not worried for her son to find a physically beautiful woman because every woman is beautiful in her own way. Physical beauty is an aspect too trivial to be a determining factor as it is constantly changing and transient while the stability of spiritual beauty determines the true value of a person.

Some believe that the cultural concept of beauty in biblical times appreciated a larger woman in contrast to the skinny woman of today. Whether you are underweight or overweight, whether you are flabby or your ribs are visible, true beauty is found within. We are what we are, as we are, and being the best version of ourselves for the glory of God is what really matters. Love yourself just as God made you—in His love.

The Bible does not give detail to the physical attributes of the virtuous woman because it really doesn't matter. *It does not matter!*

Wealth

Neither is the economic level of the virtuous woman mentioned in Scripture. Rich women are not better off for having much, nor are poor women worse off for having little. We will see that the virtuous woman has servants and does business, but this is a result of her industriousness and not of attained wealth or the inheritance through family lineage.

In many romantic books and movies, we see the opposite poles that society idealizes. The glamorous and wealthy evil woman versus the beautiful, sweet, good woman who lives in poverty. We have also seen that the suffering woman seeks success in wealth and power. We have grown up seeing that true love is found by a princess with a prince leaving most hopeless because in reality there is only a minuscule amount of princesses worldwide.

Only the blessing of God enriches and determines true worth of those who seek Him wholeheartedly. Your bank accounts and material possessions really don't matter.

Culture

Although we can determine that the virtuous woman is Hebrew by the use of the alphabet as a teaching tool, and because the general context that the Bible speaks is of that culture, we will soon see that the characteristics she exhibits apply to all cultures, breaking cultural paradigms and giving rise to the universal truth of the Word of God.

The Bible does not give preference to any given culture because it really doesn't matter.

The Journey Begins

Armed with this information, the virtuous woman no longer seems so intimidating, right? I encourage you to follow me through the pages of this book to discover the truths of the virtuous woman in your own life.

Whatever you do, do your work heartily, as for the
Lord rather than for men,
—Colossians 3:23 NASB

When I was a child and my mother asked me to help her do house-work, I got very angry. I didn't like it, and I didn't want to do it. She would tell me, "If you don't like it, then study hard so you can get a job and pay someone to do the housework. Meanwhile, do it." This response did not make me very happy, but paying someone to do what I do not like—I loved it! But it was not so easy.

It took me almost two years of marriage to get to the point where I am now and see the care of my house as a way to praise the Lord and serve my family. I never gave much attention to friends who would visit, or to the food I had to offer, or to the decor of my home. Although I did try to keep everything clean because I am aller-gic to dust, I think I did it more for health reasons than something that was born from my heart. It just wasn't important to me.

After getting married, I felt a little embarrassed because my hus-band is very, very clean in every way in the kitchen. He loves to cook, and he also cleans and washes the dishes in a meticulous way. He enjoys attending to our houseguests with dedication, and I don't—that was not who I was.

When attending a conference for women leaders in Virginia, they talked about the virtuous woman and how a woman like her, with her work at home, glorifies God. By caring for her husband, her children, her workers, and her home, she causes others to thank God for her. That changed my perspective. I thought that housework was not for me, but if it is a way to glorify God and testify as a Christian, then it definitely is for me.

As Christians, we have a testimony to keep with our families. This is seen in our obedience to the Lord and the way we submit to His will. The woman who fears the Lord obeys Him, and in doing so, her family praises her.

Alongside your effort in the workplace and your success as a professional, there are household duties that are your responsibility, and you must do them as for the Lord. Each of those duties is part of the good things that were prepared for you—do them with love, do them for the glory of God. Perhaps there is no compensation, and nobody is going to give you a prize for cooking healthy food for your family, but the Lord who sees the heart will not let your desire to honor Him go unrewarded.

The long and short of it is that either you are doing things for God, or you are doing them wrong.

Introspection

Make a list of the areas of your life in which you feel successful. Decide if these are areas in which God is glorified. Determine what is the key to your success in these areas and your motivation for doing them. There is no wrong answer before the Lord; He will guide you.

Take some time to pray and thank the Lord for blessing you. Read Genesis 39:1–6.

Who can find a virtuous woman? For her price is far above rubies.

　　　　　　　　　　—Proverbs 31:10 KJV

In my country of Guatemala, there is an abundance of jade. Because it is so common and can be found almost everywhere, it is not very valuable. The same can be said for silver. Gold, however, is not so common, and its rarity makes it very valuable. This is how the description of the virtuous woman begins by declaring her value to be above that of precious stones, which are rare and difficult to find, just as she is.

The virtuous woman is a model for us all. She is the woman in Hallmark movies or on the placards of a family used in elementary school teachings. She is that pretty woman, well dressed and with beautiful makeup, who is happy and smiling while cleaning the house, taking care of the children, organizing the kitchen, cooking, and even ironing. For a long time, I thought that this woman was only a fictional character in TV commercials or family movies. Who could be happy if they had to wash the dishes after a family dinner or had to iron pleated pants? I always thought, *Not me!*

Virtue: Excellence

The word *virtuous* is translated from the Hebrew word *chayil*, which relates to "army," "war," "strength," and "bravery." This gives us the idea of the strength required to be such a woman of great value and the courage needed to stand and to do the right thing in the times in which we live when nothing is viewed as wrong and it is offensive to say so.

In 1 Corinthians 13:13, we find what theologians call the theological virtues: faith, hope, and charity. There are also moral virtues, which can be defined as habits chosen by reason that balance between two extremes, such as right and wrong. A virtuous person then is one who has made the decision to maintain balance in all things. It has not been imposed but rather done by choice, through a commitment to excellence.

The virtuous woman, a woman of value by means of her virtues, is not influenced by the significance of any given task. She cleans bathrooms with the same attitude with which she leads a global conference. She recognizes all she does with equal importance and responds accordingly with the same interest, courage, and discipline.

All human beings must learn domestic tasks because they are a basic necessity. We all need a home; and a functional home demands cleaning, food preparation, and work in general. Let us not fool ourselves into believing that because we work for a large company or we are important businesspeople, we do not need to wash dishes and make beds. Domestic work is a necessary part of life and our obligation.

Homemaker: Single or Married

According to the dictionary, a *homemaker* is a person who manages a household. So no matter your marital status or where you live, caring for your home is your duty. Even if you pay somebody to do it for you, caring for your home is your responsibility, and you must know how to do those things to know that they are being done properly.

Putting your marital status aside and whether or not you live alone or with your parents or with friends, your house is in your care, and the details that make where you live a home depend on you. The model of the virtuous woman is found in the discipline and effort she puts into each activity she faces, be it large or small because she treats them all as equally important.

Unmarried women may only need to clean weekly or perhaps monthly while married women may need to do so more than once a week; and whereas mothers are all day picking up after their little ones, they all bear that responsibility. We must ask ourselves then, Are we doing it right? Are we being virtuous women, or are we just being women?

In the book of Proverbs, many types of women are mentioned, but only in chapter 31 verses 10–31 do we have a role model: a list of characteristics of a rare woman difficult to find and therefore very valuable. Note that this does not define your worth as a woman or as a human being; rather, it refers to the way you do what you do. Pursue excellence in all you do because it is excellence and quality of actions and attitudes that make a woman virtuous.

Value: Strength That Impacts

The Hebrew word for price or value is *meker*. Referring back to a precious stone, its price is based on weight, size, availability, and demand. If a product is not found to be attractive or useful, nobody wants it. Hence, demand decreases, and it is worth nothing. However, if a product is found to be attractive and useful, people want it; demand increases, making it valuable. A virtuous woman who faces circumstances with integrity, discipline, and excellence is in demand; and therefore, she is valuable.

The value of a person's life is great in the eyes of God and also in society. A person's life is worth a lot and is precious to those who surround and appreciate them. The larger the group of people who appreciate a person, the greater their value. Nowadays, people who have many "friends" or "followers" on social media receive proposals from large companies to use and promote their products because they know that their opinion matters to many people. The value of a person in this society is defined by the impact of their life on the lives of others. We must realize the impact our life has on the lives of those who love us.

The virtuous woman, in addition to having many things within her that make her valuable, has a strength that keeps her firm while carrying out her daily activities, impacting the lives of those around her. There is no one like her, and her excellence impacts others in such a way that they appreciate her more than anything and anybody in the world.

The challenge here is to maintain ourselves in virtue, which is the strength that will lead us to excellence in all we do. It is not an easy task, and neither is it one that we should take on alone. The Holy Spirit will guide us to the truth in the Word and will give us the strength to do the right thing.

In the face of a big challenge, a powerful resource is required. Approach God to find the power of the Holy Spirit dwelling in you, which is that resource needed to achieve everything in excellence.

Introspection

Even more valuable than precious stones is the woman who does the right thing in the right time. No doubt you have had the opportunity to be that woman, to give your time, your effort, and your things to those who need it. You have seen in yourself a little of Jesus because, despite our failures, His grace and mercy are real in our lives.

Write about an opportunity that God gave you to be a virtuous woman and in which you felt that way: more valuable than precious stones. Pray to the Lord and give thanks for that opportunity, asking for more opportunities to be who He created you to be.

*The heart of her husband safely trusts her; so he will
have no lack of gain.*
—Proverbs 31:11 NKJV

This verse begins by speaking of the heart, which is from where life flows (Proverbs 4:23). The Bible also warns us that the heart is deceitful and wicked (Jeremiah 17:9), cautioning us to take care of what we allow into it because out of it comes our way of life. Knowing the importance and value of the heart, as well as that of the virtuous woman, her husband does not take issue with trusting her with it.

The Hebrew word *leb* used in this verse to refer to the heart is not a muscle, although it pairs quite well with its vital function in our body. Neither does it refer to the heart we draw as a symbol of love, although it does have a little to do with it. What it is referring to is the immaterial aspect of the heart in which lie our understanding, our thoughts, and our feelings.

Total Giving In

Remember that the virtuous woman is the ideal woman for a king. However, in becoming a husband by choosing her, a king should not act rashly but only after careful evaluation. This husband, after analyzing the situation and the woman, decides to trust her. He does not trust her because he is blinded by love but because he understands that trusting her with all his heart is best for him. By trusting her with things of his heart, his money, his success, his projects, his family, his dreams, and his fears—he will lack nothing.

Trust is perhaps the most important element on which all relationships build upon. If there is no trust, there will be no value, and it will not last. The virtuous woman has earned the complete trust and confidence of her husband. He does not divide money; neither does he hide things, nor does he avoid her. On the contrary, he is transparent and opens his heart to her in that earned trust and confidence.

Scenario: Your husband arrives with news. Whether pleasant or unpleasant, a situation has arisen and is now on his heart. He needs to have that trust and confidence in you to be able to share. In his experience that you always receive him fully with respect and listen without judgment or interruption, he finds comfort as he shares his heart, knowing that you are there for him whether in his successes or in his failures. In doing so, you both celebrate oneness in each other as intended in God's original plan.

This not only applies to a woman at every stage in her relationship with a man—be it married, engaged, or in courtship—but also for those who desire the trust of anyone with whom they interact in their lives.

It Depends on Us

As can be seen in the scenario above, the overall outcome depends on us, how we listen. When we listen, we open our hearts as a refuge for those in need—your partner, your parents, your friends, your children. Listen without interrupting; shelter them with gestures of love and hugs. Remembering that God gave us one mouth and two ears may help us to remember that we should listen twice as much as we talk. Listening is not just an involuntary act; it is a skill to be practiced with sincerity and without judgment or condemnation.

Most every one of us would like to be our husband's best friend and hope that he would tell us everything and give us everything and not hide anything from us, but we are not willing to receive everything. Marriage is for a lifetime, and in a lifetime, there are good and bad times, and each one shapes our character and our relationship. We all have good and bad things in our being, and with that in mind, we must accept our husbands with open arms and willing hearts.

A person's heart is like a box of surprises: there will be things we enjoy and things we do not. Those that we love are those we want to celebrate and cherish, but those we do not we tend to ignore and despise. Unfortunately, we cannot choose what comes out of someone's heart, and so we must take the bad along with the good. Without any one of those little things, good or bad, the box is incomplete. If when we listen to our husband, we mock, belittle, or judge any of his thoughts or feelings, we are hurting him deep inside, in his heart. The same is true when it comes to our children, our parents, our brothers and sisters, and our friends; no one will want to share their heart with you if you do not care for it by acting with the loving stability and consistency that maintains their trust.

Sometimes we think children speak nonsense, but at their young age, they speak the truths and concerns of their hearts. However menial they may seem to us, they are important to them. The elderly, who sometimes bore us with their stories, are sharing their lives and their experiences because they are important to them, and they want to be remembered by us. It depends on us to listen to each of them with love and appreciate their trust.

The virtuous woman opens her heart to receive the hearts of others in love and never to harm them. She does not use what has been entrusted to her as leverage or a means to hurt and cause pain by divulging sensitivities or making harmful comments. She uses what she learns to positively impact her family and friends. Another version of the text says, "She will greatly enrich his life" (NLT) because it's not only about money but about all the spiritual riches that us women can bring to the life of our husband.

This is our opportunity and our challenge: that by being trusted with the hearts of our loved ones, we help them to be better, to reach their goals, to conquer fears, to overcome obstacles, and to grow for the glory of God.

Have you shown your husband that he can fully trust you? Do the people around you know they can confide in you? Trust is something that is earned by being honest, respectful, and trustworthy. By offering yourself in this way, with all your heart and with unconditional support, you will win the trust of others.

Introspection

Do you give your husband his place, listen to him, prefer him, and take care of his heart in the way you wish him to do for you? Write a letter to your husband telling him how much you love him and how you thank God for him in your life. Be specific, recalling happy memories to your mind and heart. Ask forgiveness for the mistakes you have made in your dealings with him, reminding him how much you love him. This letter is not about you or about grudges you may have; it's about earning the trust you desire from your husband and the trust your husband needs in you.

If you are single, write to a family member or friend for whom you are grateful and who has been with you and supported you in different circumstances in your life.

Thank God for the goodness He shows you in your husband.

She does him good and not evil All the days of her life.
—Proverbs 31:12 NKJV

Our passage continues by talking about the virtuous woman in regard to how she treats her husband and the process she uses in doing so. We must also remember that her behaviors are not only directed to her husband but her entire family and circle of loved ones. Although it may seem obvious that a wife should do good and not evil to her husband, family, and friends, the advice given here uses the Hebrew word *gamal*. This word describes the way she does good, which is by the process of weaning.

As the most common perception of weaning relates to the breastfeeding process, at first it may not be clear as to how it relates to doing good and not evil. By looking closer at what happens in this process, we see how a child desires only the mother's milk, and taking that away can be a painful struggle—a struggle, however, that is best for the child. The mother knows this and, correspondingly, that it will come with emotional detachment as her child is also weaned from its dependency on her. She also knows full well that during the weaning process, her child will build a lasting trust with her, as discussed in the previous chapter.

This is a truth that is important for the whole family: we may often do things that are not immediately understood by others, which cause them to feel hurt, angry, and even unloved. However, as the process plays out, our loved ones begin to understand the good that comes from our actions, and they will grow in their trust in your decisions as good for their lives. This is the trust we spoke about earlier and the way in which it must be earned.

This is no easy process for us either as we hurt along with those who feel hurt by us. The end result, however, is a happier, stronger, more loving, and trusting relationship among everyone involved. The idea of the text is of a woman who knows how to utilize the weaning process, with its inherent struggles, in doing good and not evil to those who mean so much to her.

Fortitude

The desire of the Lord is that, as a suitable help (Genesis 2:18), we may be a necessary strength for our husbands, that we be that support that sustains them when they need it. When her husband comes home from a difficult day, she does not immediately bombard him with her issues and problems, but she does what she knows will comfort him and raise his spirits: what is best for him. When her child is coming of age to eat solid foods, she does not stop breastfeeding abruptly as may be more convenient for her, but she begins the necessary process in a timely and structured way: a way best for her child.

A virtuous woman is a woman who knows how to deal with those situations that confront her and her family: a woman who does not drown in a glass of water. She knows when to listen and when to talk. She is not self-centered, doing things in her own way, but seeks the way best for those she loves. She knows her husband and family well enough to identify not only when they are in need but what will satisfy them in their time of need. She portrays that suitable help by nourishing and not being a burden or creating additional problems. This is the model of a balanced and wise woman.

By dealing with situations in a way that is best for her family, she is doing her husband good, and so she continues to earn his trust. Her decisions, her effort, and her love are for her family as a whole.

She is not influenced by selfishness, greed, or conceit but by the good for those she loves.

I insist on this because in truth the Lord called us, as women, to have great influence in our family and this is the place we must first impact. While it is important to get involved in our congregation and community, our priority should be those who live with us day by day. It would be hypocritical to give everything to the church and nothing to our family. A virtuous woman does good to her own first, starting with her husband, her family, and then others.

Courage

We all know that the majority of children enjoy candy over regular foods and can give great fuss and even tantrums when presented with a plate of vegetables. It would be easier to just give them the candy and avoid the fuss, but we know that this would not be an effective way of reaching a goal of good health; it would not be *gamal*—to deal well—in the situation. Having *gamal* as your focus, do not be afraid that your children, your parents, or other family members may get mad at you for doing what is best for everyone. We are called to give them good and not bad every day. It may mean insisting they eat fruits and vegetables, controlling television time, limiting sugar consumption, or perhaps restricting certain friendships. In the end, whatever is best, we must do because it is our responsibility to give them good and not bad.

How do you know what is best for your family? Above all, they need to know the Lord. Everything else—food, clothes, even education and friends, etc.—is secondary (Matthew 6:33). If your family is clear that God comes first and they have their faith in Him, then you can rest assured that they will learn to decide wisely and choose the good for themselves (Proverbs 22:6).

It is correct and biblical to say that the husband is the head of the household, and in love, we must submit to his authority and leadership. However, it is failing ourselves and our families to leave all of our responsibilities to him. We have been created and tasked by God as suitable helpers, and therefore, we are the best help our husbands can have. We have earned their trust in all we do by doing them good, and so we should share in that joy with them and not pile up more troubles for them to deal with at the end of their busy and tiresome day.

Do not wait for your husband to arrive so he can discipline your children. Exercise your authority and discipline them in a timely and proper manner. By leaving all discipline to their father, they may grow to fear him; his time to discipline will surely arise. Share family financial responsibilities and pay bills. Learn a skill you can do in your home to earn money and help with expenses. Find anything that is good and helpful for your family and do it.

When reading our verse in Hebrew, we come across the word used for good as *towb*. Doing good then, according to this word in the original language, demands giving the best, the most beautiful, the most pleasant. This notion goes beyond nominally providing the basic necessities by adding to, enhancing, and embellishing those provisions in a pleasing way that demonstrates our love.

Beyond cleaning the house, arrange toys in a playfully manner on the children's beds; put some flowers in a glass on the dinner table; write nice notes and put them on your husband's and children's pillows. In other words, don't just clean the house; make it a beautiful, happy, loving place to live. Instead of just packing lunches, include little notes expressing your love, a Bible verse, a smiley face on a napkin, an occasional extra piece of candy. Send text messages throughout the day letting them know you are thinking of them. Cook a special meal and dessert, or serve dessert before the meal. All these little things nourish our family physically, emotionally, mentally, and spiritually.

Introspection

No doubt we have all made decisions that have adversely affected our family in one way or another. Maybe we were angry and confused, or we deliberately did it our way. It doesn't matter. In His abundant grace, the Lord offers us forgiveness *always* and *completely*, and that is all we need, all we should seek.

Recall a time that you acted this way and confess it in prayer to the Lord. Be completely honest as you reflect on what happened. Pour out your heart to the Lord, removing all the burden of guilt. You may cry, complain, and explain your reasons and feelings. Just be honest. Jesus wants to listen to you. Rest in His forgiveness and don't let the guilt hurt you. Follow the will of the Lord with humility and obey Him however He guides you. Take actions that will benefit those you love, actions committed in your heart and based on the forgiveness that Christ gives you. How are you going to do good for those you love today?

She seeks wool and flax, and willingly works with her hands.

—Proverbs 31:13 NKJV

There are women who are dedicated to their homes yet do not want to put forth an extra effort to provide. With their many excuses, they show their lack of will to work with their hands; and to their own ruin, they find ways to get by with the least amount of effort. Tears and complaints but no effort. This is really not what God planned for us. His is a Spirit of power, not the power to manipulate but the power that enables. Fortunately, not all women are like this. Conversely, there are more who strive day by day, working and doing their best for those they love. These pages are written to all women in hopes of converting those who do not have the desire and empowering those who do.

Hard Work

This is something that I have seen in my own family with four virtuous women who I want to honor in the Lord because I have seen them work hard with their hands, in good spirits and inner desire. My mother, who despite having a difficult childhood and a not-so-good adulthood, still works with her hands and a great attitude. She travels by minibus to meet women who find empowerment through her faith, knowledge, and hard work. My grandmother, who in spite of lifelong struggles, always had generosity in her heart and was always working to support her family. My aunt, who works long, hard hours in support of my work with mission teams, also works tirelessly to bless her family above and beyond constantly maintaining her family's home. Not least of all, my sister-in-law, who in addition to caring for her husband, her children, and their home, always has a smile as she openly receives and serves more people in her home. The willingness of these four virtuous women to do what is needed in every moment inspires me.

This verse speaks of such women as these four who inspire me and perhaps to some in your own life: women who, from home—with all the chores of homemaking and perhaps with children—find time to work on something extra. It speaks to their nature by use of the Hebrew word *asah*, meaning "to accomplish or achieve something," which is what they strive for full of vigor and strength. This verse talks about a woman determined not to watch life go by but to live it to the fullest in every moment. Remember that in this passage, the woman worthy of a king is being described, and this woman is determined to give her best, *towb*, to those around her. She does not sit down to daydream but works hard for what she values in herself and her family, and in this she finds joy.

There is nothing as discouraging as doing something we do not like. It frustrates us, and we do not apply ourselves to it, thus leaving it done haphazardly. There are times when we just don't feel like doing what we know we must, and although we put ourselves to the task, we do not do it with our regular vigor. We are entitled to days like these here and there, so long as they do not become the norm (perhaps a few times a year). As virtuous women, however, we must pick ourselves up, use our hands as instruments of work, and do so willingly as for the Lord (Colossians 3:17).

Contentment

We ended the previous section by saying the virtuous woman must work willingly. The Hebrew word *chephets* used in this means "contentment, will, pleasure, desire." This is what we clearly see in a virtuous woman when she works. Contentment while working is indeed key because it awakens creativity, resulting in a more effective use of her time and talents. Contentment also comes from the satisfaction of a job well done and doing good for your loved ones.

The ideal woman for a king is a worker who does not think of herself as deserving like a princess concerned with people giving her things and waiting on her every whim. A lazy woman desires much but gets nothing (Proverbs 13:4); she has not worked hard and so neither is she content nor satisfied. On the other hand, the woman who works hard not only provides for her family but dignifies it; and in this, she finds the contentment that leads to her satisfaction. May our loved ones enjoy knowing that we strive to do them good and give them love and joy; this tells them "I love you" more than anything.

An interesting part of this verse is the use of the Hebrew word *akaph* for "hand." Throughout the Bible, it is used with other connotations as well, such as "spoon" or "pan," leaving the impression of the hand being used as an instrument. This may have been one aspect giving rise in modern culture and society that to be dignified, women must leave their homes for the workplace, where they will be empowered, respected, and recognized. However, this ideal woman works with her hands from home and does not neglect her domestic responsibilities; she uses her hands as tools to provide for her own. By saying this, I do not suggest that you do not look for a job if your family is in need but that you consider whether it is the best option. If you must work away from home, you must not neglect your domestic duties or your family in doing so. I encourage you with all my heart to consider staying at home and taking care of your loved ones because if you don't lead them to the Lord, who will? It is your privilege and responsibility. We were created with hands and given the ability to work with them.

Introspection

On a scale from 1 to 10 (1 being very lazy and 10 being very hard-working), how would you rank yourself in regard to work?

Do you like the easy things, or do you enjoy challenges and new experiences?

Do you work outside the home? If so, how do you rate the work you do? My dear friend mentioned the way we meet the challenges that come to our life: sometimes we spend much energy avoiding them instead of finding ways to overcome them. How does the word *procrastination* hit you?

Are there more things in your life that motivate you or more things that discourage you?

Are your friends, family, and those women who influence you working women? Analyze each of them individually and pray for them individually as well.

How did you work with your hands today? Did you work with contentment?

She is like the merchant ships, she brings her food from afar.

—Proverbs 31:14 NKJV

The virtuous woman, desiring the best for her family, works hard and utilizes her resources to provide them with quality products. This verse does not infer that you have to go on a trip to find those products (although if you can, why not?). Rather, it refers to doing what is necessary to offer the best we can in providing for our families. This verse uses the concept of import and export because at the time it was written, women used to spin and sell fabrics to merchants in the ports that were buying and selling items from other cities. So by selling what she had spun, she could purchase those items she desired from merchants of other cities. She did what was necessary, giving her the purchasing power and ability to choose the best for herself and her family.

Administration

As we continue to learn from this passage about the kind of woman a mother wants for her son, this verse talks to us about providing the best. She knows that a woman who always provides the best for her family will be a good wife for her son and a good mother for her grandchildren.

It is so nice that the Word reminds us that before buying, we must work willingly with our hands. In doing so, those of us who work hard can go as merchant ships, not necessarily from city to city but to myriad stores, in search of what is the best for us and those we love without going into debt.

Buying vegetables from local farmers ensures they are fresh, less processed, and perhaps chemical-free. Buying quality shoes may cost a little more, but they will provide more comfort and last longer. The idea is to do some research and make wise choices. Visit stores to check and compare prices of the same quality products before deciding. Do not settle for the convenience store or be pressured into a particular supermarket. Do not use brands just because they are the most popular. Research, compare, test, and decide the best for your family. Doing these things is being a great administrator.

Effort

Remember that the context of the passage was a time when there were no cars, and so a woman who wanted to buy had to walk, who knows how far, to the nearest port to find the best for her family. Afterward, loaded with provisions, she would walk back home happy, with a satisfying fulfillment of her ability to bring the best for her family and her willingness to go from place to place until she finds what her family needs.

We do not always have that desire nor will to go from place to place, and sometimes we just look for what is easier, even though it is not the best for our family. The key here is the happiness and fulfillment the virtuous woman finds in doing this for her family: a happiness and fulfillment that drives her to continue doing so time after time, for her good and that of her family. However, this woman is not selfish as she always gives of herself in looking to the best interest of her family. The challenge comes in knowing that if we do not give of ourselves in providing the best for our families, we will have to give more when they are in need or become ill as a result: more of ourselves and incurred expenses.

In our Heavenly Father, we see the true example of giving the best. He not only gave us what we needed but the best, even though we did not deserve it, in His Only Begotten Son. From Him, let us learn to give the best for our families.

Introspection

Sometimes we are embarrassed by the fact that we shop at the thrift store, although we may find quality products at a good price. Farmers' markets often have better products and offer better prices. Are you worried about what others think of the places you shop and the brands you consume?

Take time to do what is best for your budget and your family. In some stores, quality vegetables are less expensive while in others meats or cleaning products may be. With the cost of transportation and time, it may seem better to buy everything in one place, which it may. However, take the time to research and plan before making that decision.

Thank the Lord for the skills He has given you to make your purchases, starting with the provision of money to buy but also the ability to find the best to provide for your family.

She also rises while it is yet night, and provides food
for her household.
                    —Proverbs 31:15 NKJV

One thing that causes me to admire and respect people is the good disposition in their hearts reflected in their actions. Here I will admit to you that I do not always have it: good temperament. Sometimes I shut down around six at night because I am very tired and do not want to deal with anything, not even my phone, which I turn off. The day is over, and it is time to relax, read a book, go to bed, and get up around seven the next morning. Even so, it does not always work out for me. Being missionaries, my husband does not have continuous work, and so at times, he comes home later in the evening. When this happens, I will prepare him something to eat when he arrives. Other times he's had to wake up at four in the morning, and so would I in order to fix him breakfast and a lunch to take. Although I do oblige, I do not always do it happily. Therein lies the challenge: to do things out of love and with joy, seeing them as opportunities to serve the Lord.

A woman who truly loves her family, such as the virtuous woman, is willing to do what is necessary to maintain a loving and functional home. It does not matter the time or circumstance, if you need to wake up late at night or early in the morning or not go to bed at all—sacrifices are part of a fruitful life. Doing the right thing is not always easy, but it requires the willingness to do it, whatever is necessary. Willingness is what the Lord expects of us as believers: "For if there is first a willing mind, *it is* accepted" (2 Corinthians 8:12). If we are willing, He will use us to be a blessing.

When we study this verse in Hebrew, we come across the word *'ôd*, which describes how the virtuous woman rises in a habitual, repetitious manner, whether at night or early in the morning. In this, I see some benefits, which I have decided to apply to my life and which I wish to share with you.

1. When I wake up early, I can have quiet time with the Lord in prayer, in meditation on the Word, and in worship. This is pure fuel to start each day of my life. I am better when I spend time with the Lord.
2. Another is that at night when everyone else is asleep; there are not constant noises or interruptions. This is how I managed to write this book, working in the silence of the night.
3. I also get time for myself, listening to music, enjoying a cup of coffee, and having a time of contemplation that energizes and prepares me for the day.

This would be my ideal routine. Unfortunately, there are days in which we feel we cannot get up early because the previous days were long and exhausting. However, no matter how we feel, we must draw strength from the Lord and move on to meet the needs of our families.

The virtuous woman makes a habit of getting up before others to prepare food for her family and her maids and to assign tasks. It is very interesting that although she has maids, it is not they who are responsible for preparing the family's food—it is she. This wife of a king takes the domestic role of caring for her family very seriously. Her maids are indeed there to help, but as the keeper of the house, she is the one who gives good to her family by having maids to assist her.

It is common to have help at home, but the responsibility is always ours because the home is ours. Our maids or nannies should not raise our children, educate them, instruct them, or make decisions in regard to our home—that is our task and our privilege before God as Christian women, and we must assume it with subjection and obedient gratitude.

Having a healthy and well-cared-for family is a job that requires great sacrifice, but it is important that we be well first, not only physically and mentally but spiritually. For this reason, I encourage you to develop such a routine as to get up early when "it is yet night," and have time for the Lord—and for yourself. In His presence, there is fullness of joy, and there you can receive what you need for a successful day taking care of your loved ones.

A woman who sleeps a lot is not a productive woman. She spends her time as the lazy one who is described in Proverbs 6:9–11:

> How long will you slumber, O sluggard?
> When will you rise from your sleep?
> A little sleep, a little slumber,
> A little folding of the hands to sleep—
> So shall your poverty come on you like a prowler,
> And your need like an armed man.

A virtuous woman is willing to do what is needed for her home to be well, perhaps with little rest, but poverty will never come to her as an armed man and find her without defense (Proverbs 24:33–34).

It is not always easy to give up what we want, but for the well-being of those we love, we must "rise while it is yet night," and this can mean something different for everyone. Are you willing to stop working to take care of your family at home? Are you willing to leave your home and go to work to provide for your family? It may seem like a contradiction, but we need to find the balance that works best for our families and our situations. Can you work full-time without neglecting yourself and your family? Maybe part-time work is a better fit, or perhaps staying at home is best. You must find what is best for you, your family, and your time with God.

Introspection

The willingness of the heart is the basis of success in everything we undertake. We want to lose weight, but we don't want to exercise or forego desserts. We want our children to be well behaved, but we do not correct them through discipline. We want to have savings, but we want to keep up with our friends and neighbors or be like some families on television. We want, but we are unwilling to suffer the consequences.

You may be willing to do many things in an attempt to achieve a certain goal, but maybe not everything necessary. Perhaps you lack some discipline or perhaps the will. In what areas of your life do you need to be more willing?

Pray to the Lord for those areas that you should strengthen. Ask for what you think you need to be willing to "rise while it is yet night" and do whatever it takes. Thank the Lord for the opportunities you have had to show your willingness to do the right thing for your family.

And a portion for her maidservants.
—Proverbs 31:15 NKJV

Effective planning is perhaps the most important aspect of successful achievement. But in order to establish a plan, it is essential that we know what work must be done and, more importantly, the method of that work. With the planning and assignment of tasks comes the materials necessary to do the work. Make sure you have everything your helpers need to do what you want done, as you expect it to be done.

It is good to have help, but being able to do things yourself at home is of higher importance. Not only does it provide us with independence, but we cannot plan work for others without knowing how to do it properly ourselves. If you have help at home, it is you who will teach them what and how things are to be done. We cannot expect others to do the work to our satisfaction if they are not shown by us.

With this in mind, it is imperative that you take the time to learn these domestic duties. If you still live with your family, pay closer attention to the work being done and ask for guidance. If you already have a family and home of your own, then with greater urgency you need to learn. Read books, search the internet, ask family and friends.

Your home is your responsibility. This is one of the reasons to get up early, organize daily and weekly activities, organize shopping lists, and schedule work and family time.

Organization

In Hebrew, the original language for this passage, the writer uses the word *choq*, translated as "portion"; and this portion implies time, activities, and food. This means that those who work with you, whether at home or at work, know the boundaries and expectations set by you. They do not take advantage of your absence because you have everything organized, measured, and properly allocated. They do not linger because you have given them specific tasks and appropriate time for accomplishing them. It is not about being controlling but about being efficient and making the most of resources.

Taking care of our home, delegating by trusting in the abilities of others, resting, and planning are all skills that as women we begin to develop at an early age. The virtuous woman, who again is the ideal wife of a king, by way of her position and power, would have much control, which is why all the more she should know how to delegate, plan, and above all, how to execute each task she delegates. She does this in such a way as to continually honor her family and God with excellence.

Do not waste time. Organize, plan, make lists, notes, reminders on your phone, or whatever you need to make sure that nobody in your house wastes time and that everything will be the best possible. We must be specific in giving instructions so that there is no room for excuses or confusion in our expectations. We must be kind yet firm in what we demand without giving chance to things not getting done or not done properly. We can delegate activities, but not responsibility because in the end and before the Lord, the course of our home is ours.

When we are caring for our homes, we are serving the Lord. Your time belongs to Him, and "God is not a God of disorder" (1 Corinthians 14:33); therefore, you must serve Him with organization. Include your husband, your parents, and your children because we all have a part in the duties of the home God has provided us. In this way, you guide your family to honor God with their time and effort.

Introspection

One thing I continue to struggle with is delegating my work to others. I have a difficult time with this as a result of my controlling nature. Through much pain and application of the truths I have written in this book, I continue to learn how delegating helps me in every aspect of my life. It allows me to work on trusting others and being grateful for the help the Lord provides me through doing so.

If you do not delegate the workload and burden yourself with every task, you will most likely not do them with joy because you are overwhelmed, and you may not give each due diligence. Plan and delegate. What do you do to plan work at home? What tasks are easier for you to delegate?

She considers a field and buys it.
—Proverbs 31:16 NKJV

Even though I do not agree with the feminist movement in its entirety, I can see how important it is that women are independent and make their own decisions. These are characteristics of the virtuous woman, but she understands how to use them to care for her family and honor God. For example, she does not claim independence apart from her husband, but alongside him and in submission to his authority. She recognizes her dependency upon him, however, she uses her independence, through his trust in her, to bring good to him and their household in service to the Lord.

The Bible describes the ideal woman as a strong and independent woman who makes decisions for herself, decisions as big as investing in real estate, buying property! The Bible teaches us of a woman who works and decides on transcendent matters.

This woman, whom we have seen works for her family and who strives for the needs of those she loves, also knows how to manage her money and invest it wisely. It is not a little money; it is enough money to buy a large piece of land, and we will see later that her ambition goes big. She has worked with her hands from home and has not wasted. She has taken care of the expenses, buying in the places that favor her more in such a way that she has been able to save; and little by little, she has managed to gather a considerable amount that she now uses.

Regular transactions, such as the purchase of property, were made between men in biblical times, so perhaps her husband accompanied her, but the one who bought the property was her. That is what is told in the Scripture. Now, this purchase was not made on the run or in an outburst of emotion; rather, we read that "she considers a field." In other words, she meditates and thinks what is best for her. She analyzes the location, the work she needs to put into it, and decides. She has a plan before she makes the purchase.

Visionary

Keep in mind that she does good for her family every day, that she has the total confidence of her husband, and that is why she will not fail in her investment. She knows how to buy because she goes as a merchant ship bringing the bread from afar. And when making the purchase, she is not only seeing what she has acquired, but she looks beyond, to the work she will put into it, and to the benefits she will obtain from it. Again she has a plan and fits her decisions into it.

It is very important that we use our finances well, especially if we have little, and that our investments are not for a mere moment but that they are true and will benefit us in the long term.

If you are single, use your money wisely—*consider*. This means analyzing carefully, comparing, researching, and then deciding. Your money has been given to you by the Lord through your work, and you must use it with fear and wisdom. Do not run into investments that do not suit you just because they seem like good opportunities. First, *consider*. If you are married, with greater reason, you should consider what is good because what harms or benefits you also benefits or harms your family.

What a blessing to be able to decide on what we buy. Not every woman has that blessing, and so you must do it wisely. Invest in what is good for you without pressure, remembering that God's blessing "adds no sorrow with it" (Proverbs 10:22).

Consider also that God gives us this vision of a virtuous woman so that we learn from her so that we know that in His heart, there is no repression for women but freedom and reward for those who strive and enjoy working with their hands.

Introspection

Consider that God has control of everything and you are only the administrator of the assets that you possess. Use the Lord's wisdom to manage your resources. How do you think you have used your finances so far? Have you been thankful for them?

Have you set any mid- or long-term goals for yourself and your family? How are you working on achieving those goals?

From her profits she plants a vineyard.
　　　　　　　—Proverbs 31:16 NKJV

Something that women should and can realize more than men are the details, which are needs that do not seem necessary. They are complements, but without them, nothing is really complete. We were designed in the image of God, Creator of the human body and nature, Creator of all the different shades of green that are in the Vegetation, and who thought of every detail in all the richness of the universe. A little of that virtue of God was given to us women.

This characteristic is what stands out in this part of the verse. It refers to the work that the woman puts into the details. She goes beyond the basic needs of her family and plants a vineyard—perhaps to use its fruits for indulging or maybe as medicine for her family.

As mentioned previously, when this woman acquired the land, she already had a plan in mind: a plan for a vineyard. In order to get the full picture of what this woman is purchasing, we need to look at the Hebrew word used in this verse for vineyard, which is *karem.* The usage of this word reveals that the land for a vineyard is large as in a plantation, and this is what she wanted: a large plantation of grapes.

Among the considerations the virtuous woman made was the work needed to be put into the land she was buying. She had to clean the land, remove all the rocks from the ground, make fences with stones or thorns to protect it, build a winery, and construct a tower to monitor the plantation—hours and hours of hard work without neglecting the duties required of her every day.

Another consideration was the Mosaic Law. While a vineyard was a symbol of prosperity, the law obligated vineyard owners not to glean or pick up fallen fruit but to leave something for the poor (Leviticus 19:10). This woman saved for a long time in order to buy this land to plant a vineyard, knowing she had to make allotment for the poor; and by her virtue, she wanted to do it.

After preparing the vineyard, she had to plant it, water it, and patiently watch over the crop as it usually does not bear good fruit in the first few years. A grapevine is a plant that requires much care and patience, but after this, its fruit can be used in many ways. In the Jewish culture, they ate bread with fresh grapes at the time of harvest, and then they would let some dry to enjoy them as raisins in the winter. They also prepared a syrup or juice and made wine, which was one of the main drinks in their diet, as well as used to heal wounds.

Another consideration of the virtuous woman when making her purchase is the joyful memories it will bring her family at harvest. The Bible mentions the joy that wine brings to the heart (Psalm 104:15), not only when consumed but also at the time of the harvest. The process of stomping the grapes to make wine was typically a jubilant family celebration as families gathered singing and shouting happily (Jeremiah 48:33). Wise women worked for this joy of family memories that enriched their well-being and which required hard work and much patience. A virtuous woman knows this and considers it with the price, and she pays it because she knows that in the end, it is worth it.

This challenges us as homemakers to consider those things that are not always apparent at first but are always important for our life and our home—the details. Of course, we can live without a nice garden, but how beautiful our house looks when decorated with flowers, creating a homey environment. The basic need is to stay warm, but how much nicer with clean, soft sheets, providing more coziness. The urgency is to eat, but a well-prepared and creative meal will nourish and satiate hunger; satisfying and comforting.

Nothing worthwhile comes without a level of effort, and as we have learned from the woman of Proverbs 31, we must work for what we desire. We all want our families to be happy, but we do not need to buy land to achieve it; we must provide within our means and in a way that brings good. In whatever ways we can provide, with our love and care, we share with them the joy of the Lord in us.

Introspection

Sometimes we see what other families enjoy and would like the same for ours, but we do not know the effort required to produce their smiles. How good it is to aim for the best for ourselves and those we love, but we must have the ambition and desire and be willing to work hard with our hands. The Bible introduces us to a working woman who takes care of her family and gives them the best she can. This woman is the one we have been called to be: strong, independent, analytical, ambitious, and hardworking.

Read Proverbs 14:1–2 and 2 Kings 4:8–37.

In what areas of your life are you like the virtuous woman?

In the last chapter, I asked you about the way you work to reach your goals, but sometimes we don't have any goals at all. If you don't have any, I encourage you to set three that can be reachable and that glorify the Lord in the next five to ten years. This will help you set a vision to focus on and to manage your resources with wisdom. How exciting to start reaching our dreams!

She girds herself with strength, and strengthens her arms.
—Proverbs 31:17 NKJV

If we see something that stands out throughout the praise of the virtuous woman, it is how she uses her strength. This is not a woman who waits around for things to be given to her; rather, she is a strong and resolute woman who decides what she wants and pursues it.

Some Bible versions interpret this verse to say that the virtuous woman *wraps her waist.* This translation comes from the custom where women would tie their long, robe-like tunics around their waists like a diaper to keep it from hindering them. This was done by securing it in such a way that it was restrained on all sides. So now we have a picture of this woman who, in her determination, has removed all obstacles, thus allowing her to focus and apply herself as best as she possibly can. This is how we must approach each task we face throughout the day: remove all distractions, focus on the task at hand, and apply ourselves as best we can—just as the virtuous woman.

From this, we learn that although each moment of life poses its unique challenges, we must approach them all with the same diligence. Each may require different things from us, but we must learn how to deal effectively with them and their distractions. It is important that we use the understanding of our surroundings to deal with what hinders us and prevents us from doing good for our loved ones every day because in doing so, we glorify God (1 Chronicles 12:32). We cannot change all the things in our environment, but we can learn to handle situations wisely and free ourselves from those things that deter us, which are actually opportunities that God gives us to use wisdom and wrap our waist to do the right thing.

Firmness

Not all distractions are as easily realized, such as turning off the TV, putting our phone away, staying away from some people, avoiding certain conversations, etc. Some things may not seem like distractions at all, for instance, the myriad liberal and nonbiblical messages that emotionally bombard us daily through every sort of media. These schools of thought impart negative connotations about the work of women in the home, which may hinder us from achieving our true purpose, making it imperative that we evaluate them to determine if they truly help in becoming the woman we desire to be. Perhaps this is what emotionally hinders you, and you have not noticed. The fact is that just because many people agree on something, does not mean that a train of thought is good. You must assess everything in light of the Word of God. I pray that you fill yourself with the strength and energy that only God can give to stand firm in spite of the opinions of others, allowing you to do what God has called you to.

This verse alludes to the strength that is needed to overcome distractions and stand firm in the Truth if we want to get away from what deters us. We must be radical, willing to do what God has called us to do, and this requires emotional and mental strength, but it also means our freedom.

The strength of the virtuous woman shows not only in her controlled emotions but also in her work habits. She is not sitting around thinking; she focuses on her work. Her body and her mind are accustomed to hard work, which is why she manages to accomplish many things throughout the day. This brings to my mind a dear friend in particular, who, from the time she gets up, does not stop until the day is done, and she prepares for tomorrow. Her house is always clean and beautiful, she cooks every day, she takes care of her dogs, plants her own vegetables, goes out to hunt deer, makes crafts, and sometimes doesn't sit the entire day. Her metabolism is very high, so she doesn't gain much weight. She has incredible strength and a lot of energy. I learned a lot from her in the time she opened her house to me and my husband in a time of need, and she is truly a role model of strength—emotional, mental, and physical.

So what should we do to attain the characteristics of this woman from Proverbs 31:17?

1. Move away from what hinders us in life, be it people, places, or things, by standing firm in the strength of the Word.
2. Always be active. Physical and mental activity gives us energy to keep moving. At first, we may be tired, but the advantage is that we will sleep peacefully, and after a few days, the activity will become a part of who we are.

When you enjoy what you do, you have that spark that ignites your ideas and your heart to do everything with energy to overcome obstacles and succeed. If you apply this to the home, it makes you proud of what you do for your home and your family.

Introspection

What things hinder or prevent you from doing what you know you should do? What separates you from God's purpose for your life as a woman? How do you prepare to work at home?

It is necessary to identify what hinders us in order that we have a full life in God's purpose for us. Do not be afraid to take action, it is part of your growth in the Lord. Ask God for wisdom and gird yourself with His strength so you can take care of yourself and act for your well-being.

She senses that her gain is good.
—Proverbs 31:18 NASB

An entrepreneur is a person who organizes and operates a business or businesses, taking on greater than normal financial risks in order to do so. Although when we hear the word, it may sound trendy, the concept was not invented recently. All the local business owners that we know and the small businesses in town that we have known from our childhood are entrepreneurs.

The fact that our house is our center of operations does not mean that we cannot do more than household chores, that we cannot be entrepreneurs. Although housekeeping is our main focus, we can do other things such as sales by catalog, making crafts to sell, or the many other things we can do from our home.

Women who are entrepreneurial without neglecting their home are women who contribute a lot to their families. Their extra earnings help finance pending projects, emergencies, or simply to indulge the family.

The virtuous woman's business is doing well because she is aware of what she is doing, and she is doing it well. The idea that the first part of this verse wants to convey to us is that she verifies that what she sells is well done, and that is why she can see that her business's *gain is good*. In other words, she makes sure that things are well done for the satisfaction of others because she is the first one satisfied with the work. If she sells food, she tastes it first. If she sells clothes, she wears them first. If she makes crafts, she evaluates them first. She ensures the excellence of her work, and so too the satisfaction of her clients, resulting in guaranteeing her gain.

With this, I want to share my feelings about those who think that women who do not work outside the home are wasting their potential, their studies, their talents, etc. A woman's work at home is as important as what she does or can do in the workplace. From your home, you can bless your family, yourself, and others. The children you are raising are the future, and someday you may depend on them. Make sure they are God-fearing people and guarantee your own well-being by investing in them. May their memories of you be so full of joy and gratitude that they feel in their hearts the desire to obey God by honoring you. Some mothers expect to receive from their children what they never gave to their children. Perhaps they were selfish, and although God commands us to honor our parents no matter how they treated us, children can harbor pain in their hearts that may keep them from approaching and caring for their parents in old age. Ensure that your children receive love along with discipline.

Invest in your home and in each person within it. Share the Word of God with your family and bring them closer to Christ so you can see that things are going well with God's blessing. Investing in your family is the only business in which your investment is safe and truly prosperous.

The Lord has endowed us with many talents and creativity. Using them to start a business from home can be the solution to our desires and ambitions. If you already have a business, work diligently and remember that God is the one who prospers our effort. I hope by seeing that your business or the activity that you do is going well, you can praise God and acknowledge that your success is a reflection of His blessing in your life.

Introspection

God has given us many talents and many abilities. To some, He has given the opportunity to have a professional career; and to others, He has equipped with crafting skills. Whatever you can do, do it for the Lord. If God has given you the dream, has placed in your heart the desire, and has given you the ability to do something, don't be afraid—do it. What can you do from home? What things are you already doing? Glorify God with your abilities and put them at His service.

Her lamp does not go out at night.
—Proverbs 31:18 NASB

Do you remember the parable of the ten virgins? The Jewish tradition of biblical times was to wait for the wedding procession to pick up the bride. This practice took place at night, and so she had to make sure she had a lamp ready to make her way upon the call of the bridegroom. Of the ten, half carried enough oil to last through the night; these the Bible called wise women. The others without enough oil are referred to as the foolish. Without enough oil, the lamps of the foolish went out; and while they went for more, the procession arrived, and they were not able to accompany. Therefore, the procession passed and did not take them (Matthew 25:1–13). In this parable, Jesus stipulates the necessity of preparedness for the kingdom of God.

This verse of Proverbs depicts a prepared woman who is ready, waiting, and alert. "Her lamp does not go out at night" can be taken literally with the implication that she always had a candle lit so that in case of an emergency, she was ready to meet the need because she could see at any hour.

It can also be seen as the illustration of a woman who does not stop—her lamp does not go out. She is like the Energizer Bunny, always on the go. Her business is going well because she is diligent in her goals and in what she wants. She finds ways to improve and innovate her merchandise, so people want to buy it.

Whichever way we look at it, it challenges us to be like the wise virgins whose lamps do not go out. We do not lower our guard; we do not give up. We have at hand what we need in any emergency. Keep your lamp lit as you pray and read the Word; as you take care of your health, your marriage, your family, and honoring your parents.

Light of Life

In biblical times, oil lamps were used, which had to be constantly trimmed in order to maintain their purpose of providing correct lighting. This is the idea of a woman who is not reactive but proactive in the care of her home—constantly trimming her lamp. Lighting is a necessity for the safety and proper functionality of the home, and she does not fall short of maintaining it. The Bible is a lamp necessary for the safety and proper functionality of our life: it enlightens us when we read it, meditate on it, and put it into practice—trimming our lamp.

When our lamp is trimmed properly, we can share our light with those around us and be a blessing to them. On the contrary, if our lamp is not trimmed, we cannot be the blessing God calls us to be. A bright spiritual life begins with us and our desire to keep ourselves trimmed in the Light of life that is the Word of God (Matthew 5:16).

How long has it been since you last trimmed your lamp? When was the last time you actually and sincerely read your Bible? If you want your family to walk in the Light, you must shine it for them and guide them in it; the Light of the Word of God.

Introspection

It is difficult, if not impossible, to be prepared for everything. Accidents are accidents because we don't expect them. In spite of that, we must be as proactive as we can by being as prepared as we can. In what areas of your life do you feel more strengthened and prepared? How do you keep your lamp trimmed and prevent it from going out at night?

She stretches out her hands to the distaff, and her hand holds the spindle.

—Proverbs 31:19 NKJV

We have seen how industrious this woman is and that we can identify with her in many ways. She knows a little of everything and a lot of many things making her a woman of multiple abilities. Adding to the list is her use of the spinning wheel. The spinning wheel was a sophisticated machine in biblical times and required the ability to spin the wheel with one hand and manipulate the thread between the fingers of the other while maintaining two different and constant rhythms. She uses it to make thread, and she also knows how to make fabric with the thread she makes.

I love to see women who know how to knit, cook well, change lightbulbs, and do other home maintenance; they have their makeup bag as well as a tool bag. For these women, their hands are working instruments, and they continually use them to perfect their skills. A virtuous woman knows how to do more than one thing and is good at each of them. She does them for the Lord, and the Lord is pleased and glorified in her actions.

There are some skills that I have developed in my lifetime, but I—and surely you as well—can think of other skills to learn. Let's learn! It is not too late. This is the time to learn to do different things. Things that seem difficult and complicated can be mastered with practice and strong will. Learn to sew, cook, or bake. Learn about electrical work, computers, mechanics, and the list goes on. What do you want to learn to do? There are many places where you can develop or learn those skills you want to acquire—just do it!

When Moses began the work of building the tabernacle, God provided the skills for those who would take part in that great endeavor. The Bible mentions in Exodus 35:25–26 that textile skills were given to wise women at heart—what a great privilege. Our Creator put His wisdom in us, and we can grow and learn with His help and in His purpose just as the workers who built the tabernacle—dare to start today. A virtuous woman uses her hands as instruments of work and keeps them busy. How are you using yours?

The true independence of a woman is in her ability to fend for herself in every area of her life; this includes married women. Your husband is not responsible for your happiness or your success—you are. With his support, however, you can accomplish more, but the desire and effort to achieve fulfillment as an individual is yours.

Introspection

Sometimes we stop doing what we can and what we should because of the opinions of others or the fear of failure. I think these two go hand in hand because what we fear is the opinions of others. In reality, though, how is success determined? Will it be the amount of "likes" or the number of followers on social networks? Will it be the praise of people around us? When I determine the success of things I have done, whether fulfilled or not, I base it on personal growth and how much I learned in the process. If that is the measure, then I have succeeded in everything because I have learned and grown. With that, I leave you with the question: what makes you feel successful? With the answer comes the motivation necessary to overcome fear and start learning what you want and focus on it. Remember that if what you need is wisdom, God gives it abundantly and without reproach (James 1:5).

She extends her hand to the poor, and she stretches out her hands to the needy.

—Proverbs 31:20 NASB

A virtuous woman is generous, which is also a characteristic of our God. We can be generous because God has been generous to us. I work with poor people, and so I see the need day by day. I also see how some who have little give with joy; they do it from their heart because generosity is born in a grateful heart. When I travel with my husband for our ministry, we are hosted by people who open their homes to us with love and serve us with joy. I have experienced generosity through offering to others as well as receiving; and in both cases, it is a blessing.

The same attitude that the virtuous woman had in verse 19 when stretching her hands to the spinning wheel is the same with which she extends her hand to help those in need. Those same hands that removed rocks from the vineyard, loaded stones and thorns for the fence, and which might be blistered and scarred—are those that leave fruit in the vineyard, fulfilling the law of God to share with those who are not as fortunate. This is a great willingness that comes from the heart.

There is always something we can offer if we recognize how much God has given to us. In doing so, we see His blessings and feel the desire to share with others, knowing that there will always be more because our God provides faithfully.

Generosity does not only involve giving to the poor in need of food or clothing but giving in general to those who are in need of a hug or conversation where she offers mercy and grace and even forgiveness. Sometimes we do not need material things but perhaps a shoulder to cry on, a word of encouragement, or just a smile. The virtuous woman is not selfish and notices the needs of those around her, generously attending to them. How many times has someone helped you in times of need? How many times have you helped someone in theirs? Pay attention to the opportunities God gives you to be generous, allowing you to show His face to those in need.

Your hands are instruments of good when you occupy them in doing God's will for you in your work and with generosity.

Introspection

The Bible tells us in Acts 9:36–42 about a woman named Dorcas. She was a Christian woman who dedicated herself to giving to those in need and is an example for us all. This example does not mean that we should dedicate ourselves to helping only the poor; we must be aware of the opportunities God gives us to be generous to everyone.

In your family, there are people who have needs, and remember that it is not always material. You can also support many with your prayers. Make a list of ways in which you have practiced generosity this month.

Praise God for the generosity of others shown to you.

She is not afraid of snow for her household, for all her household is clothed with scarlet.
—Proverbs 31:21 NKJV

There is an idiom in Spanish that says "A cautious man is worth two." This basically means that when things are done cautiously, there is no need for them to be redone. As we have seen since the beginning, the virtuous woman works in this way. With her wealth of knowledge, she does things in such a way while taking care of her family that when the inevitable happens, those things were already taken care of in advance. Since she knows how to make fabric, she is able to dress her family for any situation, putting her capacity at the service of those she loves and cares for.

If it is cold, she has already provided coats. If it is hot, she has already prepared refreshments. If there is illness she has already stocked her medicine cabinet. No matter the circumstances or external factors, she is prepared—with clothes, food, and whatever else her family may need. She took precautions so she does not fear.

We take on this attribute of the virtuous woman when we anticipate situations, save by taking advantage of sales, prepare food in advance, organize what we buy, etc.

Preparation

Foreseeing implies organization, so we must make that extra effort to be prepared for whatever comes. Knowing ourselves and our family will help us a lot in preparing for their needs.

Clothing is more than fashion; it is a shelter for the body, which is the temple of the Spirit. When the rainy season is approaching, get rubber boots; it is better to be well covered than to ruin a good pair of shoes. This will also keep your feet dry and comfortable; it may minimize catching a cold and add life to that pair of shoes. When summer is coming, take care to have fresh and light clothing available. The dress code in biblical times was very important and still is. This verse refers to scarlet, which was a thick and expensive fabric used to make clothes. Having limited funds should be no excuse in being prepared for your family; thrift stores have many quality items at far less prices.

As virtuous women, we must match our style according to the needs and circumstances we face. I love sandals, but I work in the mountains where they do not provide the best protection or allow me to work effectively. Boots are the better choice that provides for my needs; I don't care if there is mud, or rain, or a lot of dust. When in the Northern United States, I am not worried if it snows because I have the right clothes for that region. In other words, we must dress according to our current needs and circumstances by using the wisdom that God gives us.

I spent the night visiting a friend's house, and in the morning, when everyone was getting ready for their day, I saw that her son's pants had a big hole in them and thought she was going to change them before leaving for school. When I made mention of the situation, my friend told me, "He is only three years old, and he is going to use paint today. I don't want him to worry, and I don't want to wash a good pair of pants. With these pants, we are both without worries."

I found this very wise. Sometimes we care more about what we are wearing than what we are doing. We must have some sort of balance. The clothes accompany us and complement us; they do not define us.

By being prepared, we take away the anxiety of the situation or circumstance. This, like everything else, requires some extra effort to think in the future, for what is coming, and act accordingly. Maybe at the moment, your household has shoes, but some are a bit worn out and the need is coming up. Think ahead. Instead of being afraid or worried, be prepared.

For teenagers, clothing is very important because they feel it gives them a sense of identity apart from their parents. In reality, though, it is only a phase, and we should support them in it without compromising our values in honoring the Lord. We must also ensure that we do not compromise our preparedness, leaving them without appropriate clothing for certain situations and circumstances.

How do you see yourself taking care of your family's protection?

Introspection

The idea that this passage gives us is of a person who knows what she faces each day and is prepared. We experience changes of seasons not only in the weather but in life, and we must be prepared. Our parents will grow old, our children will become independent, we and our husbands will grow old; and with each stage, there come changes for which we must be prepared.

How do you prepare so as not to worry or be afraid of changes in life?

She makes tapestry for herself.
—Proverbs 31:22 NKJV

This verse uses the word *tapestry*, which in many places today refers to a decoration of fabric that is typically hung on a wall. The original Hebrew word used here was *marbad* and meant the decoration of the bed: sheets, bedspreads, blanket, etc. Aside from decorating the bed, it served the dual purpose of covering oneself at night when sleeping.

Have you ever returned home after a long day, and when you got to your bedroom, you realized that you did not make the bed? How did you feel? It makes me feel terrible and, for some reason, more tired and overwhelmed. Why? For most, the bedroom is a reflection of ourselves. Your room is the place where you feel most at ease, your space of rest and privacy. When we have a visitor and need to talk about something private, we typically go to the bedroom. It is where we read, we pray, we confess, where we confide and share, and where we are intimate with our husbands. It is where we begin and end our day. It is where our attitude for the day starts to develop.

It is amazing what effect a tidy bedroom and well-made bed can have on a person. Sometimes we cover our bed with cushions and pillows, throws and coverlets, making it a lot of work to put them on and take them off—but it's worth it, right? The bed looks nice and cozy, relaxed, and in order—a reflection of how we feel.

A virtuous woman knows the importance of a pleasant, well-kept bedroom, and she spends time in this space of her home. She uses the same thread she made on the wheel to dress her family and to make the sheets with which she covers herself and her husband.

This same Hebrew word, *marbad*, is used to refer to sexual intimacy because it refers to the covering of the bed where sexual intimacy takes place. This is a part of our life that we must be sure to take care of. While single and with the fear of God and respect for our bodies as the temple of the Spirit, we must abstain from sexual intimacy in obedience to the Lord. As married women, we should treasure sexual intimacy as a gift from God in love, union, and intimacy with our husbands. We no longer belong to ourselves (1 Corinthians 7:3–5), but in the union of our bodies, we are one flesh before the Lord; and in that covenant of intimacy, our love flourishes. May our tapestries invite that intimacy in love.

May your decoration bring honor and joy to your family in gratitude to the Lord for His provision for you. Dedicate time to the things that are important, to those details that make a house your home, and in this way, you honor God and fulfill the very important ministry of being an administrator of the place He gave you to live.

Introspection

While each space in our home must be a place to honor the Lord, there are some spaces that are more special to us. For me, it is my "little room," where I read, write, work, exercise, and study the Bible. It is where I have my prayer time and where I feel most comfortable singing to the Lord. What is the space of your home that you cherish the most? How do you honor the Lord in that space?

Her clothing is fine linen and purple.
                    —Proverbs 31:22 NKJV

In the previous verse, reference is made to how the virtuous woman dresses her family. While her priority is protection by providing them with clothing, this verse makes mention of her dress code.

Appropriate Clothes

Being well dressed does not mean using the most expensive or fashionable clothing; it means first dressing appropriately. We are not going to wear elegant clothes to clean our house or to go to the park. Neither should we go with clothes that are not suitable for our age or body type. We should not dress our daughters with clothes that make them look "attractive" in the eyes of an adult, but rather modestly, according to their age, needs, and activities. Dressing appropriately is a way of respecting ourselves, our families, and our God. If we dress provocatively with miniskirts and cleavage showing, we are projecting an inappropriate image for a woman fearful of God and who loves her family.

While our desire is to look beautiful and feel good about ourselves, it is also a way of expressing who we are. We must take care not to attract the wrong attention. A provocative outfit will stimulate and attract adulterous and lustful people looking to be provoked. We cannot deny the impact of a miniskirt or revealing cleavage, so we cannot expect respect if it is us provoking others by exposing those areas of our bodies. The respect that others show me begins with the respect that I show myself.

It Is My Responsibility to Protect Myself

Many women blame others for disrespecting them when they dress in a revealing manner, and indeed, a decent man will not do so. However, a man lacking self-control will disrespect and that is the wrong attention. We cannot control the reactions of others, but we can protect ourselves against this type of behavior. We are responsible for how we present our bodies, which are to be respected as being the temple of God.

Let's face it—it does matter where you are, how you dress, and how you behave; there are consequences for everything. If you put yourself in certain situations, you should not be surprised or relieve yourself of responsibility if you encounter the supposedly undesired attention characteristic of those situations. If that type of attention and behavior bothers you and you do not desire it, then it starts with you—don't dress in a way that provokes it, and don't frequent places where it is most common. Will this completely eliminate the problem? Of course not. But it will drastically reduce it. You are more likely to get sick if you frequent hospitals and clinics, but staying away from them does not guarantee otherwise. If you do not want people looking at your bottom, then don't wear shorts with sayings on them.

A true lady does not dress to be desired as an object but to be honored. There is nothing wrong with the way she dresses because with her clothing she is respecting God and those she loves. Let's dress properly for every occasion. Sleepwear is for sleeping and remaining within the privacy of your home, not for going out to the store, to school, or to church. Seasons give opportunities to change our clothing, not our morals and decency.

A virtuous woman honors God and her family with her way of dressing.

Incorruptible Beauty

When we dress, it is not about being in glamorous attire and calling attention to ourselves as talked about in 1 Peter 3:3–5. It is about being presentable at all times as worthy representatives of the kingdom of God, as daughters of the Creator, and as heirs of His grace. Our way of dressing reflects our vision of ourselves.

The teaching in 1 Peter is the basis of the vestment of a virtuous woman, and our attire must reflect it: "with the incorruptible beauty of a gentle and quiet spirit, which is very precious in the sight of God." May our beautiful clothing reflect the beauty of our hearts. May we never look like what we are not but reflect what our Lord has done in us.

Our clothing represents us individually and expresses our education and values. It also represents our family—how our friends, the friends of our children, and those of our husbands see us. It is representative of the Christian woman in general. Let there be congruence between our inner, spiritual selves and the way we present ourselves to the world as followers of Christ.

Introspection

No woman wants to look bad. We all want to look and feel pretty, but sometimes we feel pressure from our friends, family, or husbands to always be primped. There is no pressure from God and our loved ones know how we are when we wake up. Is the dedication of your personal appearance to glorify the Lord, or is it to keep up with social trends? There is nothing wrong with primping, so long as it is proper.

Knowing the truth gives us the freedom to live in it, without burdens, without presupposed appearances, and without pressure. Bring it to the Lord.

Her husband is known in the gates, when he sits among the elders of the land.

—Proverbs 31:23 NKJV

Many women do not believe that they should be responsible for taking care of their husbands, and on many points, I agree. They are adults and should be able to take care of themselves. They should know where things are in their home, what their schedules are, if there is gas in the car, and they should able to speak for themselves. However, there are many other things and reasons for which we are responsible. When we call to mind Scripture and what God intended for marriage from the beginning of humanity—"Therefore, man will leave his father and mother, and will join his wife, and they will be one flesh (Genesis 2:24)—we are one. We reflect each other because we are one flesh. So taking care of our husbands is taking care of us. Also recall in Genesis 2:18, where God says, "It is not good for the man to be alone; I will make him a helper suitable for him."

We saw at the beginning of our passage that the husband of the virtuous woman fully trusts her, which gives him the opportunity to focus on his responsibilities. That is why he succeeds in what he does and has the respect of others. Taking care of our husbands' reputations is important to our character.

The virtuous woman's husband sits at the city gate, which during those times was the place where elders and leaders sat down to give judgment on community issues (Ruth 4). This man occupies a place of honor and can do his job with dedication because all the necessities of his house are taken care of by his right hand, his wife. How many of us want a man of leadership and power but are not willing to be the woman such a man needs (Proverbs 12:4)?

I remember the scene of a movie where a woman tells her husband's friend about his sexual impotence and other intimate matters. When the two friends see each other, everything was very awkward because he could not ignore what his friend's wife told him. We can make our husbands lose their leadership and respect for not minding our comments.

Protecting Our Privacy

Not only at work and with others, but within the family, we need to be mindful of what we say. Take care of what your children hear you say about their dad. He may be a bad husband to you, but he is their father and deserves that respect. Growing up, I had the blessing of having a wise mother who always protected my dad in front of me and my brother. Without a doubt, he made mistakes, but we never heard complaints from my mom—his wife. She always made a point to show us how good my dad was: his effort to provide, his protection, and the love he had for us. Your children need that strong father figure, and you can help them see that in their father by celebrating the good in him.

Your husband is the son of your mother-in-law, the brother of your brothers-in-law, and the man with whom you have decided to become one flesh. When you speak carelessly or poorly of him, you disrespect him and give the impression that he was a bad choice for marriage. We should definitely not lie, but we should not expose what is part of our private life. We would not like our husbands to tell others of our failures, our battles, or our secrets, and neither should we.

If your husband has a leadership position, support him, respect him, and teach your family to do the same. Remember that you are one with him; to disrespect him, whether you believe it or not, affects you and your children. If your husband does not show the leadership you would like him to, remember that God has given each person different gifts, and your desire should not be that he is famous but that he fulfills God's will for his life, which is achieved through prayer.

I want us to meditate on the kind of woman that this sort of man has. We get this from the advice a mother is giving her son about the type of woman he should seek, and this is not just any son; he is a king. This shows us that a virtuous woman is a woman worthy of being called a queen.

His Success Is Your Success

Maybe our husbands are not being the men we want them to be or the men they can be because we know they have a lot of potential. Do not compare your husband with other men; he is not any of them. Instead of making comparisons, encourage him, celebrate his triumphs (however small), appreciate his efforts, and help him see the things God gave him in order to be a wonderful man.

Do not forget that a virtuous woman is a woman who impacts the lives of others with her support and strength. Be the great woman who makes her husband see the great man that he must be. Your husband has a great responsibility before the Lord. Get down on your knees and pray without ceasing (1 Thessalonians 5:17). Ask God to enlighten his spiritual life, his leadership in your home, and his work. Your children need an exemplary father, and you need a loyal partner and a family strong in the Lord. Remember to pray without ceasing.

Introspection

Speaking of marital matters, a friend once gave me precious advice: "When you fight with your husband—and you will, like in every marriage—do not call your parents to complain about him. You will get over it, and because he is your husband and you love him, you will forgive him—but they may not." In other words, a mother will probably see the complaint as a constant issue while the wife in love and committed to the relationship will return to her husband to try and remedy the situation.

We all need to unload our hearts, and it is important to do so and not to get depressed. But we must find, with God's guidance, the right person with whom we can. This must be a wise and God-fearing woman so that she does not make gossip of our pain. This person is very important in your life, so I invite you to meditate on these questions so you can find a spiritual mentor.

Whom do you share your problems with? Who is the woman closest to your heart? (That woman may not be the friend with whom you spend the most time. She can be the person you trust the most and who listens to you.) Is she a Christian who knows the Lord? Before you run to unload your heart with someone else, do you unload it before the Lord?

She makes linen garments and sells them, and supplies sashes for the merchants.
—Proverbs 31:24 NKJV

In verse 22, we saw that this woman dresses well because she has the resources to do so. Many women lessen the family disposable income by spending on expensive designer clothes while others do so by buying many cheap things that rarely get used or don't last. The virtuous woman, however, goes beyond properly managing the family income. By doing business with the town merchants, she uses her profits to supplement it. In so doing, she becomes part of the local economy and a financial pillar in her home.

She supplied sashes, or belts as we know them today, because during her time they were very important as they were multipurpose. In addition to keeping clothes in place, they were used to hold tools, weapons, canteens, and various other accessories. Her wisdom allows her to work intelligently, using her vast knowledge to invest her time wisely in doing things of great utility and therefore of great value. She knows where she can generate more profits and knows how to do it well. Sashes were used throughout every region, both far and near; and by choosing to sell a product in high demand, she is able to guarantee herself an income.

What she can sell, she sells; but knowing that imported products are more expensive and produce higher profits, she supplies merchants who export them to other regions. She takes advantage of her interaction with the merchants as we saw in verse 14 where she brings her food from afar. She is a merchant and this is how she manages her finances and those of her home.

The Hebrew word *nathan* is used where she *supplies*, and it means *he/she gives*, and that is because she personally does the business. Her husband is respected in the community, and she has earned her place as well. She doesn't need intermediaries. She personally does business with the merchants; she makes her way in a world of men because she knows how to conduct herself professionally.

Many women say that it is a man's world; everything is designed by them and for them. There is no doubt that this is not the purpose of the Lord because He lets us see here the example of a woman who is in everything. Neither is she intimidated nor does she intimidate. Neither is she timid nor demanding because, with her professional demeanor and quality work, she earns respect. She doesn't need to act or dress like a man but maintains her identity. The world needs more women like that: women who complain less and do more—and do it with excellence.

The Lord gives us women an important place in the home, and it is His heart's desire that we love that place because it is where our feminine design works best. This does not, however, prevent us from going further and being part of the business world that seems prevalently male-driven so long as we remain faithful to our purpose in the Lord and maintain our God-given femininity. We see women like Deborah, Jael, and Abigail who armed themselves with strength to defend their homes and their people in a male-dominated world. But with God's blessing and faithfulness to Him, they saved many. Not that as women we should remain in the home but that we respond to the needs of our home first and not give up our femininity to be involved in activities that require a male role.

Some women who succeed in male roles have given up their femininity. They reject it by going against their very nature and assuming roles that do not correspond to their design and dishonor God as well (Romans 1:26–32). Some do it to prove that they are equal to men even though we were not created to be equal but to complement each other. This will never be the purpose of the Lord for us; His call to our lives will never go against what His Word teaches us.

Do not complain about how the world is perceived; find your place in it. Show by your actions what God gave you to contribute to this world so that your work is recognized and respected wherever it is presented. Whether at home or in the workplace, in whatever you do, you can make a difference by providing ideas and doing quality work that impacts and inspires those who see the results of your effort in faithfulness to God.

Introspection

I am not much of a businessperson, but I come from a family of businesspeople and have seen how in a community everyone benefits when quality work is done. How do you contribute to your work environment? Do you honestly consider your work to be quality? Are you being faithful to God's design for you in femininity and faith?

The advice and inspiration of the world are confusing. Approach the Lord and give Him the doubts that may be in your heart. Go to the Word and find His Truth for your life in its teaching. You are a woman, and as such, you must honor the Lord. Talk to someone if you feel confused, and never follow the world and its confusion. Find light for your path in the Word of God. Read Psalm 19.

*Strength and dignity are her clothing, and she smiles
at the future.*

—Proverbs 31:25 NASB

This verse states that her clothing is made from nonmaterialistic things. No store is able to sell strength and dignity, and neither is any manufacturer able to make clothing of them. So then what does this mean? As we saw in the previous verse, we use our clothing as a part of our identity, and so we can see here that a virtuous woman identifies with these things—strength and honor. She focuses on those garments that do not go out of style and that come from an Eternal God.

She strives and does everything for God. This shows us that, although taking care of our physical appearance is important, only by working on our dignity can we become virtuous women. It is a spiritual exercise that gives you such assurance of who you are in the Lord that you can laugh at the fashion trends that routinely come and go. Your confidence becomes eternal, founded in strength and honor.

Her Clothing

We talked about how well dressed this woman is and this verse focuses on what 1 Peter mentions: the clothes that don't go out of style, those of the heart. While this reference to clothing is not something that is seen, it is something that radiates from the depths of our hearts. It makes us shine without using fancy accessories of gold, silver, and diamonds. A confident woman can wear the simplest clothes and look regal. *Hadar*, the Hebrew word used here for "dignity," refers to the honor that allows her to do business with men, selling her goods, and buying land. They don't do business with her because she is pretty but out of respect and honor. She respects them, and they honor her.

As women, we have always cared about what we wear; and being no surprise to God, His Word makes this illustration that brings us an important truth: *your confidence is linked to your concept of eternity.* What you believe is valuable defines your lifestyle and priorities, so you must evaluate everything you do in the light of the Word of God, guided by the Holy Spirit. A virtuous woman has her foundation in the eternal things; it is God who dignifies her.

While she takes care of her reputation and that of her family, she is not worriedly thinking of what others will say about her because her interest is in the honor she receives from the Lord and her family. The standards of the world have lowered to a point that people are praised for doing what is expected of them—the minimum. A dishonest and unethical society in constant decline and denying its own nature cannot recognize right from wrong or good from bad. The virtuous woman cares more about what God thinks of her. Honor and recognition of her strength and dignity are important to her only in the Light and Truth of the Eternal God and not in societal standards.

The Future

In this way, we who have been dignified, forgiven, and redeemed by Jesus Christ, can live confident and assured that what is coming can only bring us closer to the presence of God. With a smile, we can expect the fullness of joy that is only found there with Him.

If our concept of eternity is not based on the Bible, our way of life will be focused on earthly things that will surely pass away (1 John 2:15–17). If our concept of eternity is based on God's promises in His Word, then we know that in the future the glory of God's presence awaits us.

In this verse, the word *smile* comes from the Hebrew *sacha* and means "laughing with mockery." When new schools of thought make their way into society, she is not worried. She is amused because she knows that there is nothing new under the sun (Ecclesiastes 1:9). Her house is founded on the Rock (Matthew 7:24–27). Her values do not change because her strength is immovable and invariable (James 1:17).

Fashion trends come and go so quickly and often; and many, after a time, return. The fears and doubts of today will be replaced tomorrow by other fears and doubts, but those who wait on the Lord renew their strength and hope that motivates us to live in purity (Isaiah 40:31). Do not be distracted and confused by the constantly changing world around you, but choose the good part like Martha's sister Mary and find strength and honor at the feet of Christ (Luke 10:38–42).

Introspection

We all care about the opinion of someone—usually one close to us. Why do you care? What makes this person's opinion so important to you? Do you admire this person, and if so, why? What qualifies them to be critical about things in your life? Do you think their opinion is close to that of God's?

Many people are sent by the Lord to guide us, educate us, and help us grow in Him, in His will, and in our life in general. Sometimes we admire people because we see them as pillars that God has placed in our congregation or community. Do you think that person whose opinion you care so much about is sent by the Lord for your growth?

She opens her mouth with wisdom, and on her tongue is the law of kindness.

—Proverbs 31:26 NKJV

Contrary to the associations of feminist advocates and non-biblical worldviews, the virtuous woman is not a submissive woman who remains silent to the point that she lets herself be taken advantage of. Above all things, this woman is wise. She does not speak nonsense, nor does she let her emotions cloud her judgment. A virtuous woman speaks with self-control, and that attributes to her greatness.

Wisdom, according to the dictionary, is "knowledge or learning gained over time," and that is what this woman has. She is informed, she cultivates her mind and intellect, and she does not stop learning as we read earlier. She uses her wealth of knowledge to advance in personal growth, and that is why she shows prudent conduct in life and in business. Even when she gives orders and instructions, she speaks with kindness and with the manners of an educated person—like a lady.

Self-Control

She has developed the great strength required to manage her tongue, which is a small member that does a lot of harm if we cannot control it. According to James 3, if we are able to control the tongue, we can control ourselves in every way. When we talk, we reveal more

She watches over the ways of her household.
—Proverbs 31:27 NKJV

This verse makes me see two very important things: One would be encouraging all the women who stay at home to let them know that they are not wasting their time and potential. And second, to raise prayers for those who work outside their homes because this responsibility of watching over their households did not disappear when they signed a contract with a company. The truth that this verse reveals to us is linked to wisdom in the previous verse, and its relevance transcends cultures.

Here, this verse does not speak merely of the things of the home but also of those with whom we share it. In other words, we must always be aware of what goes on with our families within our home. This does not mean meddling in the privacy of others but carefully observing the actions, attitudes, and demeanor of our loved ones: who they spend time with, their relationship with the Lord, their activity in the church, their academics, their work performance, etc. With a simple and kind question, posed as we read in the previous verse, you can know what happens with your family by paying attention, as do watchmen in their rounds, which is what the Hebrew word *tsapah* used here indicates. In fact, this word also refers to the action of leaning forward to see something carefully, as if inspecting it. That is the quality of care that our families need. Remembering how organized this woman is, it is no wonder that she would know when something is out of place or when something is not right.

Our Family First

We must speak wisely and help them to understand and achieve what is best for them. Whether it be your husband, your children, or even your parents, you must speak the truth to them with respect, love, and with wisdom. The virtuous woman watches over them with love; their lives are still of your interest. Even if you work away from home and come home tired, you need to find time to serve the people that God has put in your care with love, respect, and joy.

Our home is our first ministry, and we must ensure the welfare of all who are part of it. Sometimes we give a lot of ourselves outside our homes, being successful in our careers and serving in church with enthusiasm, which is all good, but our households may be falling apart. When reading 1 Timothy 3:4–5 regarding overseers, we see the importance of managing the home related to serving God, and so this must be done as our priority. In other words, if we cannot manage our homes, how can we manage those things God has given us, such as the business we do to supplement our homes and help others? Other businessmen and merchants will see us in the way we manage our lives. Whether our husbands serve in the church or not, we must manage our homes in the sight of God, subjecting ourselves and our households to the morals and values taught us in the Bible.

Taking care of our families first means monitoring what they see on television, what they spend their money on, what they do with their free time, etc. It means guiding them in their fears and ambitions and knowing how we can be the support they need. How can we do any of this if we do not pay attention to them or "watch over their ways"?

I want to encourage you with all my heart to look for resources that create an atmosphere of warmth, love, and joy in your home. The enemy is trying to destroy the family by changing what God intended for it to be: the design of marriage, between a man and a woman; the nature of man and woman, letting children decide their gender identity; the concept of parenthood, wanting to be best friends instead of parents or treating pets as children. With all of this and more, the enemy is abolishing our Christian morals and values. The battle is real, and we must be prepared to face this sad reality. Greater is He who is in us, and only with His help will we be able to keep our families strong and united. Remember it is with His help and guidance, and this is why we must always be in the Word—preparing for battle.

Femininity

Femininity is the characteristics or nature that makes a woman a woman. It is a gift from God to us women, and we must celebrate it. Our sensitivity is not weakness but strength, and our limitations are not disabilities but opportunities—both allow us to rejoice in the purpose of the Lord. It is an insult, to real women and to God, when a man believes he can become a woman through surgeries and hormone pills, neither of which can ever give a man the femininity that the Creator designed for women. You can put lipstick and pearls on a pig, but it is still a pig. Femininity is God-given, and we must defend it and celebrate it.

We are not like men. We were not intended to be, we cannot be, and we should not want to be (and neither should men try to be women). We were created to live with and complement men through our divinely given role as women, and pointing it out is not an insult but a wonderfully uplifting fact. Who decided that being a woman is any less than being a man? The passage of 1 Peter 3:7 has been misinterpreted to put women in a lower place than men, and this could not be further from the truth that God intended for us. This Bible verse refers to the physical and emotional differences between men and women, and no doubt men are naturally stronger. However, before the Lord, we are all the same as we see the same verse instructs men to honor women as fellow, or equal, heirs of His grace. We were created in love and sensitivity, to be loved, supported, and respected. The best that God could create for man is in us, and we must defend that privilege and responsibility.

Let us teach our young girls the richness and fullness of femininity, to love their role by design, and to be proud of who God created them to be—women. Let us help them see their true nature, the characteristics that God has placed in them, and the grace that makes them the perfect balance to be a worthy woman before Him and others. May their understanding of themselves always be based on the Word of God.

Masculinity

As we again draw attention to the treatment of the weaker vessel in verse 7 of 1 Peter 3, we must teach our male children that their role as a man is the protection of that vessel, as well as leadership in the family. If a woman adopts the position of authority and leadership in the home, it is because the man has fallen short and not fulfilled his role. When the man gives up his responsibility in the home, it becomes a survival instinct that forces the woman to assume it in the same way that if a bus driver becomes incapacitated, somebody will immediately take the wheel to avoid catastrophe. It is not the other person's natural duty and, if left long enough, will eventually lead to some other type of disaster, just as when the man never reassumes his position in the home. This is also a form of abuse to the woman and is most certainly not God's plan, which the young men must learn in your home.

Let us teach our young boys to be gentlemen, to open doors and carry things, and to be helpful—chivalry is not dead. Teach them to collaborate in the home and to make wise decisions with the help of God. That is what being a man is all about. We need to teach them that to be a great man, they must follow Christ because their responsibility before Him is great. They are to be the head of the family, but Christ is the head of them, and only guided by Him will they fulfill their purpose in life with success (1 Corinthians 11:3).

Some people believe that we should not tell children whether they are boys or girls and that they should be allowed to decide for themselves later, when they are ready—this idea could not be more absurd. This can be proven in transgenders who stop their hormone regimen and begin to transition back to their original gender. If you have to take medication to maintain a condition, that condition is not normal. It is our responsibility to ensure the intended moral stability of our home; our children are not born with a sense of right or wrong and need our guidance. They cannot even control their sphincters, much less understand their role in life without proper moral guidance. Men and women were created to complement each other, and that is the sense of community that was designed into the family.

Watching over the way of our home is not only about seeing what is wrong, but it also gives us the opportunity to honor the good things done by our children and our husbands. The opportunity to celebrate their triumphs and strengthen them with love and grace in their weaknesses is ours. Accept their friends at home and be an example for them of a confident woman who loves her family for the Lord.

Marriage

This is also an opportunity to take care of our marriage. Outside our home, our husbands are exposed to temptations, and the enemy does not rest, especially if we have a husband who wishes to please the Lord. The aim of a watchman was to prevent dangerous or harmful situations. He could see from afar if there was an impending threat and gives notice to those under his protection, allowing them to prepare to face the danger or perhaps avoid it altogether.

These days, cell phones and social networks can be a danger to you and your husband: reunions with old friends or hiding conversations with people who should be avoided. Flirtatious chats and suggestive pictures are instruments of the enemy attempting to destroy our homes. They may seem innocent to you or to him, but they are not. While you should not invade the privacy of your husband by checking up on his phone or computer, you should be open and honestly discuss these issues with him and, above all, pray.

As watchman of your household, you must be able to see the danger and act accordingly to defend your home. Put on the armor of God and ask Him to guard your husband's heart and mind and give him the strength in the Spirit to be the man that Christ desires and that you need (Ephesians 3:14–16).

With the wisdom that the Lord gives you in His Word and in prayer, you must face the threats against your family. Do not remain in doubt. Clarify situations with love and grace so as not to give rise to thoughts that lead to incorrect decisions and actions.

It is not an easy task to be the watchman of your home, but it is your privilege before the Lord. Be then the warrior, full of courage, that the Lord designed you to be as a woman. That is our call, and that is the responsibility of a virtuous woman.

Introspection

Having doubts can become obsessions if we do not clarify them and jump to conclusions. We may think our children or husbands are hiding something, and by making assumptions, we become paranoid and suspicious of everything. This is something we must avoid! We cannot live under the same roof without mutual trust. The solution is to bring things into the light and ask without accusing—remember how to speak from verse 26. That is the point: that in order to do so, you need to put on love, which is the perfect bond so that there is no more conflict, only solutions (Colossians 3:14). In other words, in order to clarify, we must first question; and before questioning, we must pray. Then we must listen, and before listening, we must pray—and multiply it all by love.

The formula to do this is:

$$\text{Clarify} = \text{Love} \times ((\text{Pray} + \text{Question}) + (\text{Pray} + \text{Listen}))$$

But above all these things, put on love.

And does not eat the bread of idleness.
                    —Proverbs 31:27 NKJV

The second part of verse 27 talks about laziness, and when viewed in correlation with the first half of the verse, we can immediately see the implications. If the watchman is lazy, then he will not be aware of the surroundings and thereby put the household in danger. Among the myriad dangers resulting from this are waste and debt.

The original text uses the Hebrew word *asluth* in this verse for "idleness" which is translated as "sluggish" or "slow-moving." For example, when we first wake up, and we lack that coffee boost. During this time, we are not fully functioning, move awkwardly slow, and need some time just to get ourselves going. Unfortunately, as implied from this verse, for some, it does not end there, and this is how they move throughout the day—it has become their way of life. Let's take a look at the two dangers mentioned above that can result from this type of lifestyle.

Waste

For the most part, waste is a by-product of laziness as a result of wasting time. Wasting time prevents productivity that can be used to profit our households. Wasting time does not mean doing nothing. To the contrary, it involves doing other nonessential things with our time that lead us into non-desirable situations. As we waste our time on such things, we compromise our homes and families. We put them in situations they do not deserve, and we confuse their ideas of a correct and godly family life. Wasting time can usually be found as the root of many of our home and family problems.

Look after your household with the honor and privilege bestowed upon you by God. Remember to do it, like all things, as doing it for Him (Colossians 3:23). Do not endanger your family and household by wasting what God has given you to take care of them.

Debt

To understand one way in which laziness can create debt, it is necessary to paint a picture. When someone is lazy, they do not take care of necessities and typically will replace them with other things that will cost more than if they had been done. For example, instead of taking the time to grocery shop, they will contact the delivery services of the stores from which they have need. Instead of cooking a well-balanced meal, they will order out (having it delivered), go to a restaurant, or fill the freezer with frozen dinners. With all the available services these days, it is a battle to prevent ourselves from falling into this trap of laziness. Many times, this type of living will slowly drain our finances, leaving our families vulnerable to any compromising situation that comes along, and we have put them there.

Another thing that can happen is that with the time we should have used to grocery shop and cook dinner, we may start watching more television and spending more time on our phones, which can lead to unnecessary spending. For example, the infamous "one day only" and "limited-time countdown" sales which create impulse spending without regard to our financial condition. These are temptations created by vicious marketing organizations that know many people will follow the impulse; they have no concern about you or your family.

Be mindful of what you spend your money on and always think whether you have the funds to pay. Are you spending your money wisely? Many people rely on bonuses, which they have not yet received, to pay debts created long ago or to justify incurring new debt: money that could have been put into savings or used for a family necessity. Just because something is on sale does not mean you are saving money if you don't need it or buy more than you do need. A frugal life is a life that leads you to get the most out of what you have and to buy with great intelligence.

Work

There is one Bible translation that I find interesting that reads, "She does not eat bread that she did not work for." It leads us to think about the dignity of our life through work. If you live taking advantage of others and you have not earned what you eat and what you feed those you love, you must change your attitude. Respect yourself and respect your family. Work for what you want and need. Be wise. Strive with the power of the Lord for what you desire. Work and do not let idleness cause you to beg.

By being manipulative and abusing the kindness of others or helpful organizations, we may manage to get what we need, but our children are learning to be lazy. This leads us to the core of this passage.

Laziness

This does not mean not doing things because of being tired but because of the lack of will and desire to strive. Of course, the virtuous woman gets tired. She achieves so much by taking advantage of every moment of the day that she surely sleeps peacefully as a result of exhaustion from so much work. But she does not use that as an excuse to wait until 10:00 a.m. to get up every day, and she knows that if she did, there would be so much left undone by the end of the day.

Laziness is neglecting the things we are obligated to do: the lack of will to do what we know we have to. Regardless of whether it is an easy task like serving coffee or moving rocks out of our field, we just don't want to do it. We want wine and grapes, but we are not willing to be productive and earn them.

Not eating the bread of idleness also impresses the idea that she does not engage herself in what is not profitable and does not waste her energy on nonsense. Take, for example, the futile discussions in social networks where we spend so much of our time and effort only to get angry, frustrated, and confused. We get caught up commenting and contributing to intangible debates that waste our time and alter our mood and therefore our productivity. This is a total lack of wisdom resulting from laziness.

When we act concerned about other people's situations in order to avoid facing our own realities, it requires a lot of effort. We are being presumptuous busybodies as a result of eating the bread of laziness, and this is what we are feeding our families. Remember that we must provide them with good and not bad.

We cannot deny that we have all had moments of need and required someone's help to get out of a problem, and that is not bad. God has put us in our communities for that reason. His desire is that we help one another. However, when receiving becomes a way of life, when you do not strive to stand in the way God intended, and when you feel deserving of the hard work of others—you are sinning. You are not loving them as yourself, which is what Jesus gave as the second great commandment. You are sinning.

Introspection

Our work dignifies us. We saw that the virtuous woman dresses with honor because she has earned the respect of others with her hard work and wisdom. I know several women who feel a deep commitment to being watchmen of their homes, and they do not want to get a job. This seems great if they have a husband who shares this idea, but some refuse to work and have put their family in need. They don't want to make the effort required to earn their bread. What do you think of that? How do you dignify your life through your work?

If you have been one of them, have no fear. There is grace in the Lord and the opportunity to be redeemed. New are His mercies every morning!

Her children rise up and call her blessed;
Her husband also, and he praises her:
"Many daughters have done well,
But you excel them all."
—Proverbs 31:28–29 NKJV

Our home is our safe place, where we feel most at ease. It is where we are perhaps more of our true selves, without makeup or heels, but in comfortable clothes. Comfort is not only exterior but also interior. When we are at ease, we tend to express ourselves with more spontaneity. Those who live with us, seeing us on a daily basis, know us best. What does your family think of you?

I have seen many people trying to get along with everyone except with those whom the Bible gives specific instruction: their immediate family (children, wife, husband, and parents). These are the people who are ultimately going to be there for us in hardship. There are parents who even teach their children to lie because appearances are very important to them—more than the truths that are lived in the privacy of the home.

Transparency

We can feel great satisfaction if we have the admiration of colleagues at work or of the people of our church and community, but what is that if we have a home where we are not appreciated by the people closest to us, who really know us? In the end, we always return to where we belong, and that is the place where the Lord wants to nurture, encourage, and recharge us so that wherever we are, we fulfill His purpose for our lives.

This truth is hard to share and much harder to apply. Remember that our first ministry is our home, and so the first people to whom we must show love are the members of our family. More than once, I have had to stop my work, pray, and ask the Lord for forgiveness. I had to ask Him for humility and wisdom and then go apologize to my husband. I don't want him to hear me preach what he doesn't see in me, and I don't want him to hear from my mouth what he doesn't see in my actions (Matthew 5:23–24).

This does not mean that we should not do anything for others but that, while we do for others, we must always continue doing for our own. True love comes from those who truly know who we are, who know everything about us, both good and bad, yet continue to love us. This is the love that the Lord has for us (Romans 5:8). And true honor is given by those who, while knowing our faults and mistakes, decide to recognize our strengths.

The praise of those who see us from time to time is a bit empty when we analyze it well. How much can a person I see once a week really know me? However, sometimes we settle for that, as with the "likes" of social networks where people only see what we allow them to and which many times we embellish with photographs and stories. This happens because we have not kept a testimony in our home that holds us in high regard. Instead, we have hurt those we love and so do not receive from them the approval we need as human beings. We have passed on God's approval in the belief that we have failed Him and allowed guilt to get in the way.

The Bliss of the Right

A virtuous woman does not suffer these things. Perhaps she may experience misdirected anger, undue tantrums, and unjust rejection of family members, but when the time comes, her children get up as if to recognize or defend her and call her "blessed." This comes from the Hebrew word *ashar*, meaning "guidance," which is indicative of the important role she plays in their lives. However, it also translates as "happy" and "blessed," which is how she feels in that role. According to many Hebrew scholars, the idea of this phrase is of a person who is well balanced, able to do the right thing and be happy.

They recognize how their mother has worked for them, suffering long days. They know the way she wants them to walk because she has disciplined and corrected them. They are aware of her love that has led her to give them even the simplest things. They understand the wisdom that she has because they have heard her speak and maintain her respect. They know that she is the guide in life that has led them to Scripture, so in obedience to God, they honor her.

The Bible does not specify the context in which her children call her blessed, but they could be setting her as an example in conversation, mentioning her in a speech, publicly recognizing her industriousness and strength, or defending her against slander. In any case, how beautiful to know that your children will refer to you in that way—calling you *blessed*. Maybe right now you are going through a difficult time, but that will pass; and if you stand firm to what is right in the Lord, you will have the blessing of children who recognize your strength and balance and refer to you as blessed.

Suitable

Her husband is not far behind. When the children go to bed and she ends her day, she goes to her beautiful bed to rest, and the last one who sees her is her husband. Feasibly, like most of us, they have a little conversation before bedtime. Perhaps she tells him of her plans and projects with emotion. Maybe she listens to him carefully as he gives her wise advice and encourages him to continue. She is happy with what happens in his life, and he is with everything she has done during the day. Afterward, she falls asleep peacefully.

This man has seen her in the best and worst of her days. He has seen her honoring God, heard her daydreaming, and watched her making plans. He has received her comfort, her support, and her guidance. He has listened to her complaints and has seen her failed attempts. After all this, he knows that he is also *blessed* because, out of all the good women available, he has the best one for him. Seeing her among other good women, women who will respect their marriages and care for their families, he sees things in her that surpass them all—she honors the Lord. He does not want more than she can give him and knows that she will not give him any less. That is why she is always in his heart. To him, she excels them all and is more valuable than precious stones.

When we obey the Lord and seek Him first and wholeheartedly, He guides us. He takes us to the center of His will, which is good, pleasant, and perfect. There, He gives us the precious gift of a suitable mate. The best person we can find is the one God gives us. That is why we should not go anywhere looking for anything else outside of our marriage; we will not find anyone better suited for us because none other will be from the will of God. The husband of this virtuous woman is not looking for anything else outside his home because there he has everything he needs. He is sure that she is the best for him, and he praises her for caring for their home and family in every way she can.

On a good day, marriage requires constant effort and work. This is why we must not stop praying for our husbands and why we need God and His Word in our hearts. The Lord's desire is for our partner to lift us up and love us deeply and unconditionally, in the way that He loves us and gave Himself for us (Ephesians 5:25–33). If your marriage is in tension and there seems to be no solution in sight, I want to remind you that there is a solution, and it is found only in Christ. You must get down on your knees and not give up. Through the power of prayer and in God's time, you will be praised by that man whom you love and lifted up daily before the Lord.

The virtuous woman is celebrated by those who know her best and love her most—her children and her husband. Compared with all the others, she excels and is the best for them. Each child should believe in their heart that their mother is the best, and each husband should recognize that among all women, the most suitable for him according to the grace of God, is his wife.

Introspection

It is the desire of my heart that you feel appreciated by your family. More than that, however, I pray that in the depths of your own heart, there is no doubt that you have done the right thing—not in your opinion or that of others' but according to what the Lord demands of you (even if for a time your family is unable to recognize it). I pray that when the time comes, your children can say something beautiful about you from their hearts and that you receive it with an open heart and not in vanity. May your husband always find reasons to praise God for your life and thank you from his heart with love and kindness.

Take a moment to thank the Lord for your family and for the occasions when they have shown you their love and respect. Praise the Lord for that blessing.

Charm is deceitful and beauty is passing,
—Proverbs 31:30 NKJV

Something that excites me is to see the beauty of large women in television commercials, shows, movies, magazine articles, etc. It seems that the concept of beauty is becoming increasingly broad and inclusive, and that is great. It gives the opportunity to look, feel, and be beautiful to all kinds of women because we all have that right and privilege. In fact, the Bible says in Ecclesiastes 3:11 that "God made everything beautiful in its time," so regardless of stereotypes, God put beauty in every woman. Unfortunately, society continues to place emphasis on physical appearance as the most important aspect of a woman's beauty.

Appearance

This verse uses the Hebrew word *chen* for "charm" and refers to favor or graciousness, which is closely linked to the attractiveness of a woman. The other Hebrew word used here to tell of the deceitfulness of charm is *sheqer*, also meaning "falsehood" or "lie" and conveys to us that this appeal is not as real as it seems. It is a type of graciousness that enchants or *charms* people deceitfully because it has no foundation. It is like the confidence that many women have which comes from their desire to look and feel beautiful. However, it is only appearances: an external beauty that has no congruence with the interior of a person. It is misleading and influences the way others perceive them—through a lie.

We live in a society that encourages women to be rebellious, contentious, strong, and confident in themselves and celebrates these behaviors as a form of attractiveness. The Bible teaches the opposite, and so this type of worldly attractiveness is deceptive. All these supposed strengths are illusions if they are not grounded in the Word of God. Only trust in the Lord remains and transcends. The beauty that celebrities reveal in their personal primping and accessorizing and in their relationships, publicizing great weddings and adventures with pictures of seemingly incredible happiness and that receive thousands of "likes"—but with marriages that last only weeks or days. This is the deceitful charm that this verse speaks about.

A person who is anchored in the truth of the Lord, who speaks truth and wisdom with firmness and conviction, would not be very popular these days. Charm *is* deceitful. Greetings and comments that are not born from our hearts but make us look good in front of others are deceitful charms.

Useless Investment

The second part of this verse talks about physical beauty, everything that is perceived with the natural eye: an athletically defined body, shiny hair, bright clothes, and everything that presents to us an idea of glamor and beauty. The Hebrew word used here for beauty is *yophi* and is also used in Esther 1:11 when King Ahasuerus calls for Queen Vashti to show off for her *beauty* to the guests at his feast.

This is an artificial beauty that is overly encouraged in our society with modern technologies and advanced makeup techniques and procedures that help a woman look like a completely different person. The beauty industry, with total disregard, pushes state-of-the-art exercise equipment, experimental diets, and surgeries that create health risks to many women every year. Reductions here, increases there, and a few tucks all to try to be who we are not because that is what we are told we should be and causing us to want to be.

Unfortunately, none of it can change who the Lord created us to be, and in the end, there is but an empty being—an unsatisfied soul.

Of course, there is nothing wrong with beauty and personal care. However, we must honor God in our body (1 Corinthians 6:20), and that's the key, the motivation to take care of ourselves. A heart more concerned with what others think than in the opinion of God does not give Him glory. We sing to the Lord that He is perfect and wise, but in what we do with our bodies, we purport, "He was wrong with the nose he gave me. The surgeon can give me a better one." We play god. Pride and the desire to win the approval of others is not the right motivation to take care of ourselves. The bodies our God gave us and how He sees us is *beautiful*.

Investing time and money in a form of physical beauty which does not glorify God but is focused on gaining people's admiration not only puts our health at risk; it is investing in something temporary—a useless investment. This Scripture tells us that this type of beauty and attractiveness has no value. Remember that what is valuable is difficult to find. Everywhere you look, you can find tools and procedures to create this beauty that is not worth much. It is temporary and fades away (Ecclesiastes 1:2).

To fight against time is a useless battle. We cannot control time, only what we do with it. Time causes us to age, which is part of God's plan for us (gray hair is the honor of the elderly [Proverbs 20:29]). There is no cream, wax, or injection that can stop what God has already arranged, and any attempt to defy it is to go against His will. We are but dust; we cannot defeat His plan. A virtuous woman does not waste resources by fighting losing battles; she uses them to invest in her family, in her home, and in her old age being dignified by the work of her youth.

Introspection

How much do you care about physical beauty and whether people like you?

It is normal for us to be concerned about looking good and having a good reputation. We must do it as representatives of the kingdom of God. But sometimes we lose sight, and it becomes vanity, perhaps only a little at a time, but we grow to like it. If this is something that we see has become an obstacle in our relationship with the Lord, we must turn from it, and only with the help of the Lord Himself. Approach your Heavenly Father humbly in prayer. Tell Him how much you love Him and how important your relationship with Him is in your life. Tell Him you want to change and ask His help to do so.

But a woman who fears the Lord, she shall be praised.
—Proverbs 31:30 NKJV

The virtuous woman is a strong woman as can be seen in that the Hebrew word for "virtuous" can also be used in reference to an army. No doubt this woman has warrior strength as the Lord of hosts leads her battles.

A virtuous woman knows who she is in the Lord. She knows that her strength is in Him alone and in the way that He uses her in the good works He prepared for her. Everyone wants to be God's masterpiece, but not necessarily to obey and follow His will (Ephesians 2:10). God's will for women is that they find their value in Him and not in themselves or in others.

Women who follow liberal and non-biblical thinking want to instill independence in other women: a confidence to do whatever they want because they believe they can. The Bible teaches us that we are dust (Genesis 2:7), and apart from Christ, we can do nothing (John 15:5). So they may think they have done it all themselves or with the support of other like-minded women; but if Christ is not recognized as the only means, and that without His sacrifice on the cross we are lost, it is a sin, and their destiny is eternal torment in hell. Without Christ in our lives, we only find sin. He is our only hope because while we were sinners, He gave His life for us (Romans

5:8). In Jesus Christ, we find purpose, and that purpose is to glorify God (Isaiah 43:7).

We need God. When we start building a house and do not know where to start, we go to the architect who designed it, and he gives us the plans. Now we know where to start and every step along the way. We are God's design. When we don't know what to do at any point in our lives, we need the plan: His Word. Only then will we have the correct guide. I say correct guide because just as we would never think of using the plans from some other house halfway through construction, we should never use any other plan than the Bible for our lives. We must seek God—He is our architect.

Fearing the Lord

Fearing God means recognizing who He is and His greatness. It means approaching Him according to who He is and what He deserves. The fear of God should ignite in us the desire to be close to Him, to please Him, and to obey Him.

When we were children, my dad had a temper. My brother and I feared him. We didn't want to cause trouble, and we did our best to be obedient. We knew that he loved us and that he would protect us from danger, but we also knew what should happen at what time and this created discipline in us. In the same way, knowing God allows us to know what to do and when to do it; it instills respect and disciplines us in our words and actions. John 1:1 tells us that the Word is God, so only by reading the Bible can we meet Him and know who He is and what He desires of us. By spending time with Him, in His Word, your love and reverence for Him will grow and you will become a woman worthy of praise.

A woman who fears the Lord shows Him her devotion in all aspects of her life. She does not focus on vanity nor is her charm deceptive. She follows the truth and that is her foundation. Her ability to organize; attend to her husband, children, and servants; work hard; keep her house in order; do business; have time for herself; and reach out to her neighbor flows from her intimate relationship with God. God is the source of all good, and those are the things she focuses on (Philippians 4:8).

This verse reveals the secret of the virtuous woman. After all we have learned about her, no longer is she so intimidating because now we know how we too can be virtuous women. The revelation of becoming the perfect woman worthy of a king is fear of the Lord. There is hope for us. If we are close to God, we can organize, prioritize, and succeed—but only after we draw near to God (James 4:8).

Introspection

Devotion is a sign of strength. A person who is devoted to Jesus must deny themselves, and this requires self-control. Whoever has control has power, so a woman who has a deep devotion to the Lord is a powerful woman.

Where are you spending most of your time? That is the source of your honor. Are you spending your time in social networks or in the Word? Are you trying to know more about celebrities or God?

Daily time with the Lord is very important. I know that for me, it is the fuel and refuge for my soul. When I fear my own thoughts, I find comfort in the Lord. The desire of my heart is that you learn to put God first and start living a life that glorifies Him because only there will you find purpose and true contentment.

Give her of the fruit of her hands, and let her own works praise her in the gates.

—Proverbs 31:31 NKJV

The virtuous woman has honored God and worked hard her whole life caring for and blessing others. Now has come the time when she as well is deserving of the blessings she has poured out through her lifetime. She does not need the admiration or approval from the men of honor at the gates—her lifelong works speak for her. She is at the point in her life when she can look back and see all she has done and can now sit back and enjoy the results.

Throughout her life, and even more so now, she is known by how she lived. She doesn't have to explain herself to anyone because she has demonstrated the truth and what she believes through her actions. Nobody can reprimand her for finally, at this time in her life, slowing down to enjoy what she has spent her life creating.

Too many women do not live as the virtuous woman does, and so they never get to the point where she is now. It is not enough to say "This is who I am" or "That is what I do" because the truth comes out in what we actually do with our lives. If you say you are a Christian but you do not act like one, are you? A picture is worth a thousand words. But you contend that you diligently go to church. Unfortunately, going to church does not make you a Christian any more than sitting in a garden makes you a flower. How you live your life is your testimony, not what you say about yourself. Do you live to show your love for the Lord?

The virtuous woman has worked to show her love of the Lord, and so she receives His reward (Matthew 6:4); she can now partake of the fruit of her hands. She strived all her life to earn her position, worthy of honor and love but in humility. In her wisdom, she knows who she is and how she got there—living for the Lord.

The praise you receive from what you do within your home and outside your home is for the glory of God. This is the testimony of your Christian life. Through your life, you speak of your love for the Lord and your relationship with Him. Out of that love, you instruct your children in fear of Him and treat your husband as He desires. No one can go without noticing the goodness of your heart, your smile, and the general well-being that you have because you live in the fullness of joy that is found only in the presence of God.

Our lifestyle says a lot about us; it is our testimony. A life guided by the Spirit is a life that shows bold faith, without fear, and without yielding to the pressures of others. People respect a life that reflects strong and sincere convictions. In the context of this verse, we see that the virtuous woman's lifestyle of spirituality and convictions testifies to her before the prominence of the city gates. Her intention was not to gain public praise; but through her selfless lifestyle, living for God and for her family, she is finally able to reap the benefits and receive praise in her humility (1 Peter 5:6).

The Word says that our Father, who sees in secret, will reward us in public. This reward will come from the lips of people who will encourage you to continue working for good and to honor God. If the praise focuses on your work or on you, it is not the Lord's reward. In my many years of working in ministry, I have received words of affirmation, offerings, invitations to teach, cards, and even gifts as signs of gratitude from the people I have served. While the glory is not for me but for the Lord—and I always say it because I believe it—I know that people realize the heart with which you do what you do. These people challenge me to be the person God made me to be: a woman who brings praise to the glory of His Name.

We may not be where we should be, but it is my prayer that in this book, you have found the necessary exhortation to move forward, the desire to grow, and strive to be the virtuous woman you were created to be. I pray that you have learned not to live according to anyone's standards but according to the strength and power that you find only at the feet of the Lord.

It is my desire that as Christian women, we commit ourselves to serve the Lord so that everyone sees the difference in our lives; that we do not settle for what everyone does because we were called to shine; and may that light that shines through us guide others who see it to salvation in Christ Jesus (Matthew 5:16).

Introspection

At the beginning of this book, we made a list of things that make us feel successful and analyzed the motivation of each one. Now, in light of what God has revealed to you in these pages, I invite you to reevaluate that list and identify all the things that give you success as a virtuous woman before God. Let us thank God for the wisdom He has given us to act virtuously in those areas and ask for strength to continue growing in Him.

Only in Christ!

While writing this book and meditating on each part of this passage, I have realized who I am in relation to the virtuous woman and why I have an innate desire to be as much like her as I can. I have also come to believe that all of us have this same desire within us because that is how God created us—to be strong, brave, and virtuous women. It is quite a challenge, especially with the inundation of worldly pressures, to be such a woman, and that is why we must devote ourselves to God in all things. It is not that we must attain all the virtuous attributes at the same time but that we recognize our need to be such women—and that we continually strive to that end so we can be what we need to be in the right time and with the wisdom and strength of the Lord.

Not all lessons throughout my life have been easy, and some are challenges not yet overcome. Others have been a comfort to my faults because I know that the good that is in me comes from my Heavenly Father. I also know that those things in my life that are not right and must change are in His hands, and with my obedience, He will finish the work that He has begun in me (Philippians 1:6). We are a work in progress. Some days we go fast, and others we go slow, but the important thing is to continue on the path of good works that God planned for us in Christ.

After seeing myself in contrast to the virtuous woman and seeing how much I need to grow,

- I take refuge in the grace of God, who loves me and gave Himself for me;
- I comfort myself in knowing that my God, who knows all of me, loved me and will continue to love me and will give me His fullness to live the abundant life that He offers me in Christ Jesus;
- I rejoice in my weakness because when my strength fails, I see God's great power leading me to where He wants me to be;
- I commit not to lower my guard or conform to this world but to continue changing my way of thinking to follow His will and, as a virtuous woman, speak wisdom, which is the Word of God;
- I continue working in my life and in the Light of Scripture, which is the absolute Truth of God, knowing that only in Him there is hope for this life and eternity.

This list of points are steps that I have come to realize I must take in order to submit to God's will. Hopefully, after reading through this book and participating in each introspection, you have come to a similar realization of your need to grow and the steps that you must take to do so. Many of our steps may be the same since we are on the same journey with the same ultimate goal, and so I encourage you to incorporate any of those you feel will help you get closer to being the virtuous woman we have learned so much about.

Commit to the Lord, and let's take on this journey together. Let's impact our families with femininity and strength in the glory of God.

Thank you for taking the time to read this teaching of the Lord for every woman and for learning to be the woman God wants for your husband and the mother God wants for your children: the woman your community needs. Remember that apart from Christ, we can do nothing.

My Testimony

I grew up in a culture of male dominance, where abuse by men happens in broad daylight. A culture where women did not condemn their abuse but justified it.

Many women have grown up like this, following patterns that put them at the beck and call of abusive fathers, husbands, and children. Many women promote this machismo culture and male abuse to maintain their "suffering woman" status, which they feel makes them more dignified before God. It is as if they were paying penance within their own families.

These women, who defend the abuse that victimizes them, have the greatest responsibility in the family. They have to juggle finances to cover all expenses that may arise, and they bear everything "for their children." It is also they who criticize single women for not marrying.

In my childhood, I never fully understood what was happening, but I always knew deep down that something was wrong. I would hear in the church of a God who does good but wondered why He let men be abusive and treat women the way they do. There was no congruence, and I had a lot of confusion. I did not dare to ask. But, as protected as I was, I noticed that it seem to be the norm.

The Lord gave me many Bible verses and songs to take refuge in and much faith to believe in Him, even though I didn't see Him very often with all that was going on around me. Eventually, the Lord intervened in my life and took me to a place where He restored and healed me.

The Lord gave me the opportunity to know and love Him, and with the strength of His love, He helped me break through cultural patterns by surrounding me with wonderful people who modeled a Christian life. I wanted that life, and the Lord gave it to me—not as I expected but as He in His goodness wanted.

I know that God's purpose for women is not the abuse and victimization that I witnessed in my childhood, but neither is it the empty empowerment that the world demands through geographical and generational culture. I consider myself a countercultural woman because I was called to go beyond the expectations of my culture as well as those of being born a millennial. I know there is a balance in virtue and that it can only be achieved in the Lord. In my own life, I have seen how Scripture is the light at my feet and how it has guided me. I am confident that the same will be for you if you decide to submit yourself to the Lord because only there we can find the truth for our life and the strength to live it as it was intended.

To break cycles of oppression, we must be in the Word every day, pray without ceasing, and sing to the greatness of God. These are the three things that have led me to a life closer and closer to fullness in Christ. I thank God for making me a woman and giving me purpose in Him to be countercultural.

Appendix

Do Not Remain Silent

Silence is one of the worst enemies of abused women. Perhaps out of shame, you are not talking about your situation, and this is understandable. Nobody wants to accept the role of victim. However, that silence only chains you to the abuse that victimizes you and perpetuates that cycle of pain. Talk, denounce, ask for help—don't remain silent!

Abuse doesn't just mean hitting and physical assault; it includes all kinds of attitudes and actions that hurt you and make you feel afraid. In true love, there is no fear (1 John 4:18). So regardless of whether it is a relationship of a couple, family, or friendship, if you feel intimidated, you must break that cycle of abuse and that emotional and mental violence.

Violence can also be verbal. When rude words, insulting nicknames, or conversations are used to hurt you, you should walk away. Ask for help. Do not remain silent.

Maybe fighting would be a bad idea, but asking for help will never be. Despite your need to speak, you should not and cannot speak to just anyone. Be wise and look for these characteristics in the person who will help you.

- *A woman.* The situation you live in makes you vulnerable, and entering into a relationship with this degree of confidentiality with a man can end up confusing your heart.

Even if he is a pastor, ask that his wife be present. Never talk about this alone with a man.

- *A woman who loves the Lord.* Although many people can give you advice, only a Christian who loves the Lord can give you what you really need: Christ. Also, she will be prudent and will not share what you entrusted to her with anyone else. A person who loves the Lord will guide you and motivate you to act in a way that will help you and glorify Him. He is our Rock, and we must run to Him.

- *A person who serves in the church or community.* Although all believers must help others, not all of us have the gift of service, and you need someone to help you concretely. A Christian who loves God will at least pray for you, and that is a lot of help. A person with a serving heart will do more for you because it is her inner desire to help others with her actions and resources.

Prepare yourself. Speaking will not be easy, but it will be the only way to find freedom. In the process of breaking cycles, we will have pain and dark days, but the Lord will make His face shine on you all the time. Even if you do not see Him, believe Him.

Do not be afraid, do not feel worried, do not feel ashamed, and do not remain silent.

For My Children

Some women believe that they should remain in the relationship of abuse "for their children." However, this attitude only places on the little ones the burden of avoiding problems between the parents, giving them a responsibility that not only does not correspond to them but is damaging their hearts.

You may not notice it, but your children are very well aware of your relationship with your husband. Perhaps it is better for their own well-being that they see their father for less time and that that time is of quality than to listen to disputes that put tension on their hearts and expose them to mistreatment after a strong fight between the parents.

Your daughters will take your example. Do you want them to suffer what you suffer? Your children will repeat the patterns they see in their home. That's why there are abusive children in schools because in homes, we are allowing abuse, and they are learning it. The abuse does not stop over time; it only reproduces.

Children's behavior is a reflection of parents' behavior. Children need a stable home, and this does not mean all remaining together while suffering abuse; it means peace and harmony. If your children see you suffer and cry and then hear that you continue in that relationship of pain for them, they immediately receive the blame for your pain when the decision to continue there has been yours. Teach your children to take care of themselves and walk away from what hurts and harms them by your example.

A wise woman said that we should not worry that our children do not pay attention to what we say because they are paying attention to what we do. Model conduct of dignity and respect.

My advice is not divorce but the emotional and physical security of your children. It may be necessary to put space and time between you in order to resume your relationship with your husband in an environment and with measures that are appropriate for you and your children.

My desire is that you see your children as the great treasure they are (Psalms 127:3) and do not use them as an excuse to be with who you want to be, or expose them to the threat of abuse that you have decided to cling to. The Bible calls us not to provoke our children to anger (Ephesians 6:4), and guilt is a cause of anger and a source of pain for them. Guard their hearts.

As a daughter, I can say that a mother's suffering is not alien to us. Many children are victims of the inconsistency of seeing their mothers being abused at home and then seeing them celebrate their abuser in public. This pain causes anger, depression, anxiety, and a riot of emotions that only destroy what we should protect.

Your children need a father, but they also need a happy, worthy, and loving mother. Do not hide in them. Arm yourself with courage and decide to stop the abuse with time and physical distance.

Seek help from a woman whose family loves the Lord and who can help you without negatively affecting her own family, maybe a member of your church.

Remember that your children are your responsibility and that by putting physical distance between you and your husband, you will be working for their well-being, and the work will dignify you in their eyes and before God.

The time of separation is not a party of spite and moral shame; it is a time to reconnect with the Lord and His purpose for your life and your family. It is a time to:

- Spend time in prayer and the Word.
- Maintain a good attitude.
- Don't complain in front of your children.
- Don't neglect your personal presentation.
- Pray for your husband.
- Don't stop going to church.
- Do not allow your children to make disrespectful comments.

Maintaining distance is a lot of work and requires strength, but without a doubt, the result will be a blessing for you and your family if you do it with the fear of God.

Singleness

Singleness is not a sentence for your lack of something. Especially if you are a Christian, you should walk with the assurance that Christ gives you by having enough in Him.

Happily married women will tell you not to worry, that the right one will arrive in time and that it is worth the waiting. Unhappy married women may tell you never to marry and hate all the men in the world because "they are all the same" as the one they chose.

However, I start with a question: what is God's purpose for your life?

Married, if you do not know who you are, you will be a completely dependent wife who has nothing to contribute and who will have to remain silent, because if you do not know what to do in your own life, how can you have an opinion in the life of another person or a family member?

I encourage you to focus on yourself. This is the time when you should know yourself and do what you can to love yourself and enjoy each moment in your own way because once you get married, it will no longer be your way. It will be the way of two, and that individuality that we have in singleness will not exist anymore—and should not exist—because now the two are one flesh. We will continue to be us, but now we are making decisions as a couple, and it will not always be 100 percent as you want.

Singleness is a time to grow in the Lord, to take positions that will keep you firm in times of crisis, and to prepare what you are going to offer to the man that God has for you.

Do not wait to get married to fulfill your dreams because those dreams are yours, and how fantastic if your future husband shares them. But if not, you will be frustrated. There will not be someone who is just like you, and that is a lie that the enemy has put in our way to keep us from finding the partner that God has for us. There is no one like you; only you are you. Your future husband does not have to come full of gifts or money to give you what you want (but for which you do not want to work). Nor does he have to come to make you happy because happiness is built with each decision; and if you put all your expectation of happiness in the love of your life, you will receive the disappointment of your life. A husband does not bring

- happiness,
- economic security,
- personal fulfillment,
- identity,
- worth,
- purpose.

All this is found in the Lord and holding His hand, you strive for all that on your own with His blessing.

We must work for our happiness, to enrich ourselves in all aspects, to be suitable, to be the perfect help for our husbands. And that is what you should focus on while being single, in being so happy that you can give happiness, in being so successful that you have sufficient to share, in making yourself so wise that you can decide, and in loving God so much that you truly fulfill God's purpose for your marriage.

I know there are days of solitude and that seeing our friends together as couples make us feel "more single," but despair will only take you to a place of total pain and frustration. I know that the enemy and society make us believe in love as that happiness that makes us smile without stopping, and sometimes it is. But I also know that if you are not happy with yourself, you will not be any happier with someone at your side. I know that family and culture put pressure, but none of them will live your marriage, only you. I know that many men seem right, but only one is the one that God has for you. Wait for him patiently in prayer and in preparation.

Know yourself, love yourself, strengthen yourself, sanctify yourself in the Lord; in other words, prepare yourself. Marriage is a mystery, full of joy and blessing; but even on a good day, it requires hard work.

If your future husband comes into your life today, what do you have to offer?

About the Author

Author Photo by photographer Elliot Morales

Mimi grew up in a male-dominated country and trying to break those cycle of dominance participated in feminist movements during her time in university. For her commitment to Christ, she attended Bible Seminary where she graduated as a professor of theology. She has dedicated many years to working with women of all ages in different countries and cultures, teaching God's plan and purpose of love for women in conferences and through her online magazine *Camino a la Plenitud* (Path to Fullness).

Today, she and her husband are full-time missionaries serving those in need out of love for Christ through their ministry Straight Path Ministries you can contact her at mimi@straightpathministries.org.